Endorser

"Rachel's sincerity and deep love for God come through in every word of *Finding Jesus in the Wilderness*. As someone who knows her personally, I've witnessed her integrity and faithfulness firsthand. In this book, she offers vulnerable reflections from her own wilderness experiences. This book is a rich treasure to help the reader lean on Jesus and find hope, even in the driest seasons of life."
Steve Uppal, senior leader at All Nations, Wolverhampton

"Honest, rich, vulnerable, powerful… This book ministered to my soul, and I know it will again. I really believe we are in an hour of the Lord making a way in the wilderness; He is transforming and calling His Bride so they are ready to stand firm in Him in the days to come. Rachel's words help us not to lose heart but know the Lord's hand and purpose in every season of our lives."
Anne Calver, *Unleashed* overseer

"*Finding Jesus in the Wilderness* communicates with clarity how purpose can be discovered in pain. So often our deepest purpose is discovered in our greatest pain. Wilderness seasons are more common than any of us realize. We can easily begin thinking something is wrong with us when we are facing a wilderness. Yet, as this book demonstrates, the perfect Christ himself faced a wilderness. As I read her manuscript the various stories and analogies really resonated with me. Rachel writes about this topic with honesty, vulnerability and unique insight that I sincerely found to be encouraging and refreshing to my soul."
Lawrence Neisent, lead pastor of Destiny Christian Centre, Oklahoma

FINDING JESUS

in the wilderness

40 Reflections for Dry and Difficult Times

RACHEL YARWORTH

Dedicated to God, who has always been faithful
to bring me through my many wildernesses.

And to Aimee, who God loves so much He made it your name!
I am so thankful He sent you to be my sister and friend xx

Contents

Introduction

IN GEOGRAPHICAL TERMS we use the word 'wilderness' to describe an area of unpopulated, uncultivated land that is often dry, barren, and without the familiar comforts we love. It is an analogy that most Christians will relate to at some point when we find ourselves in a spiritual wilderness – a season when our walk with God seems drier and more difficult than we'd previously known. Wilderness seasons are unpleasant and deeply uncomfortable, but each one is a journey that every Christian must eventually travel as we mature in Christ.

As you are reading this book, I am willing to guess you may be in a wilderness season of your own, too, or at least have experienced times like this in the past. Hold on – help is at hand.

Each wilderness experience is unique. Some are deliberate, like during Lent when some Christians fast, depriving themselves of certain luxuries and comforts in order to connect with Jesus' forty days in the desert. Other wilderness times are triggered by specific difficulties such as sickness, bereavement, trauma, or other painful experiences, when troubles make the love and blessings of our Heavenly Father feel far away and out of reach. Yet other seasons seem to come out of nowhere, and we somehow come to feel we have lost the joy and closeness we used to enjoy with God.

At the point of writing, I am also in my own wilderness season. It is not my first, so experience gives me reason to believe God will work through it for good: I am not without hope. But this time it has lasted over two years, and even though I have received some signs that it could be ending soon, it is still a difficult and painful place to travel through. So, when I felt a prompt from God to write this book while I am still walking through it, I realised it was important to Him that the voice you as readers hear is not one far removed from the experience, written through the sanitised rose-tinted filter of hindsight, but a voice of authenticity that honestly owns some of the intense difficulties experienced here. Just as Jesus went through His own wilderness experience so we would have a Saviour who understands ALL our struggles, so I believe He wanted me to share my own, with the hope that His voice and mine will offer companionship and hope through the season you are facing.

In one sense it is impossible for any of us to physically take this journey together: each person's wilderness season is one that God has mapped out just for them for the purpose of deepening their relationship with Him. I cannot and do not want to interrupt that. However, in my own wilderness journeys God has revealed to me many treasures to be found, including people from the Bible who travelled this wilderness land before us and learned valuable lessons in their most desperate times. As you read through this book you will meet many of them, each of whom dwell in different parts of the wilderness and are able to reach out a hand and help you navigate their particular area of experience.

You will notice I have given the chapters headings that relate to specific difficulties and wilderness paths. You are, of course, welcome to read through the book in the order it is laid out, or do feel free to refer to the contents page and find the chapters that relate most to the place you find yourself, as no wilderness path is neat and linear and each person's trail will follow different routes. The places mentioned in these pages are some of those most visited in the wilderness, and it is my heartfelt prayer that you will be helped by the ones who have gone before you.

You may wish to treat the book as a daily devotional, particularly if you are following the Lent tradition. Or you may prefer to read a chapter and then sit with it for a few days, allowing the Holy Spirit to speak deeply to you in that area for however long it takes. For those who keep journals, I have also published a companion prayer journal at request from some of my beta-readers. It contains quotes, Bible verses, and questions to help you dig deeper and focus in on what God says to you through this book, with plenty of space for you to write your own thoughts down. You can find it at my website (rachelyarworthwriter.uk) or on Amazon.

One last thing to notice: the chapters are evenly divided, alternating between the difficulties and the hope found in the wilderness. If this is your first wilderness experience, you may be surprised to discover the treasures here are every bit as significant as the pain and hardship. There are blessings here that cannot be found anywhere else. And I hope this will be your first encouragement: the wilderness is uncomfortable, lonely, painful, and difficult, but God will redeem your time here, and in the end, it will turn out to have been utterly worth it all.

I cannot make this season any shorter for you, but if I can help you to find Jesus in it and to know you are not alone, I will count it a true honour. God bless you richly,

Rachel

PS Some of the chapters in this book contain words that I believe I received as God's communication to me/us. These words are in *italics* to help distinguish them from my own thoughts, but they are not intended to be granted the same infallible weight as words from the Bible – the truest survival guide ever. For more information on hearing God's voice, see Appendix 1 at the end of the book.

Chapter 1 – Place of TEMPTATION

"Then Jesus was led by the Spirit into the wilderness to be tempted by the devil."
Matthew 4:1

FOR ANYONE TRYING to get to grips with a wilderness journey, I believe this passage is the best place to start. Because Jesus is our Lord – the One we desire to follow – His own experience of entering the wilderness is a must-read. Whether we have entered this season voluntarily (e.g. through deliberate fasting), or it has come to us another way, it is comforting and inspiring to know that Jesus Himself experienced it before us.

At the time of our opening Bible verse, Jesus had just been baptised by John in the Jordan river.[1] It was a symbolic act: unlike every other person who has ever been baptised, Jesus had no sin to be cleansed of, but His baptism marked the beginning of His ministry. It showed the point when, identifying with humanity, He officially 'died to self' and embraced the call to lay down His life in service of God's Kingdom – the original model of Christian ministry. He descended beneath the waters, and as He emerged, "Heaven was opened, and he saw the Spirit of God descending like a dove and alighting on him. And a voice from heaven said, 'This is my Son, whom I love; with him I am well pleased.'"[2] So, the Father, Son and Holy Spirit were all present together at the start of Jesus' ministry: a significant, glorious moment!

But rather than take the opportunity to launch a public campaign announcing the Saviour of the world complete with God's divine stamp of approval, the Holy Spirit immediately led Jesus into the wilderness. Talk about contrast! One minute Jesus was glowing with public affirmation from His Heavenly Father; the next, He was walking into a lonely, dry, and barren land where He would be physically and emotionally starved for the next forty days. It must have felt confusing and disorientating. I wonder if He felt a bit like me in my own wilderness seasons, wondering if I had taken a wrong turn somewhere along the way, and asking 'how did I get here?'

But was Jesus being punished for something He had done wrong? Clearly not: Father God had just said He was very pleased with His Son. Was His visit to the desert a result of Him neglecting God? Again, no: He had just embraced baptism as an act of obedience. In truth, the Holy Spirit deliberately led Jesus into the wilderness because it was an essential point in His life, without which He would not have been fully prepared for ministry.

So right from the outset I want to say to you, if you are experiencing a wilderness season right now, please do not beat yourself up, feel shame, or blame yourself for being here. There is a strong likelihood that the Holy Spirit has led you here because you are being prepared for the next stage of your life and/or ministry, as Jesus was. You might think your visit is the consequence of wrongdoing on your part, but there is still strength, growth, and treasure here God wants you to find that you will not find anywhere else. So, let's keep looking to Jesus as our guide through this difficult time.

When Jesus followed the Holy Spirit into the wilderness, He was led to a place of temptation.[3] Most of us will experience the same. Even those who deliberately choose to embrace a form of wilderness through fasting (more on that in Chapter 9) will likely be tempted just as much

---

[2] Matthew 3:16-17
[3] Matthew 4:1-11

as those who unwittingly find themselves here. For when we experience seasons of hardship, the enemy is always right there tempting us to find an easier path. Our physical bodies and our souls crave comfort, not lack, and temptations land more easily when we feel deprived.

One main thing all Jesus' temptations had in common was the same thing that the enemy tempted Adam and Eve with at the beginning of time. In fact, all temptations, including our own, come down to the same thing: the temptation to reject God's way and follow our own will. 'Eat the forbidden fruit and become like God,'[4] 'Turn these stones into bread and eat,'[5] 'Worship me and I'll give you glory and fame,'[6] 'Take this shortcut to avoid suffering, and do what feels good to you', etc. It all turns us away from God and towards self-serving.

And, as Jesus showed, the way to overcome any temptation is to reject our own will and to submit to God's.[7] Adam and Eve listened to temptation and gave in to what seemed better to them, rejecting God's words, but Jesus did not. He countered every self-serving temptation with "it is written",[8] putting God's Word above His own desires. That is how we resist too.

When I read accounts of Jesus' temptations, or watch dramatised versions, it often seems like the devil had a visible body that Jesus argued with – that the temptations came from an external source. Whether or not that is true, the much more common experience for most of us is that the temptations seem to be coming from inside ourselves, sounding like our own thoughts and feelings. They feel far more subtle and insidious than if we were arguing with a visible talking snake. This is why the Bible says to "take captive **every** thought to make it obedient to Christ".[9] We must learn to examine our thoughts

---

4 Genesis 3:1-5
5 Matthew 4:3
6 Matthew 4:8-9
7 Matthew 4:3-10
8 Matthew 4:4,7,10
9 2 Corinthians 10:5 – emphasis mine

and feelings, recognise which of them line up with God's truth, and when they do not – when we catch ourselves feeling or thinking anything contrary to God's word – we need to learn to stop, acknowledge that it is not God's truth, and then choose to live by God's truth instead, however hard it is. This is the process of learning to resist temptation that Jesus demonstrated.

It's easy to say, but so much harder to do. Putting this into practice over every thought is one of the hardest but most powerful lessons I address in every wilderness season. I know God's Word is true, and I want to live by it, but I still often feel like succumbing to self-pity, irritation, impatience or bitterness. I still find myself trying to take control and find my own way out. Especially in dry and difficult times, my emotions constantly try to take over my thoughts and decisions. You probably know the feeling too – so it's comforting that even the apostle Paul said, "I have the desire to do what is good, but I cannot carry it out. For I do not do the good I want to do, but the evil I do not want to do – this I keep on doing. Now if I do what I do not want to do, it is no longer I who do it, but it is sin living in me that does it."[10]

The fact is, resisting sin is hard – really hard. We can't just pay it lip-service; we can only learn it by experience. So, these seasons of temptation may feel tortuous, but they are essential to our growth as Christians. They expose the self-indulgent sin within us, so that we can learn to deny self as Jesus demonstrated and become more like Him.

Holy Spirit, help me learn to resist temptation as Jesus did, I pray.

---

[10] Romans 7:18-20

Chapter 2 – Place of REST

As I sat with my family on the patch of grass surrounded by rock and bracken, gazing across the beautiful autumn landscape encircling Rydal Water far below, my heart sank. Almost – but not quite – at the top of Nab Scar in Cumbria, I had to accept I was not going to make it to the peak. It had been a long climb, and I had been repeatedly spurring myself on with thoughts of the view from the summit, but the scree-covered slope ahead was steep with no handholds, and vertigo was kicking in badly. Even after a stop for lunch the dizziness was still not subsiding, and I reluctantly conceded that this time the safest and wisest option was to retreat. I was sorely disappointed. Quitting is not something that comes easily to my stubborn nature, especially as this climb had been my suggestion, and we had come so far – I was so close! But wisdom prevailed, and I began the journey back down with my tired younger children, leaving my husband and eldest son to do what I could not and make it the rest of the way to the summit.

It may have been wise, but still, it felt like failure. The sense of achievement after a hard climb and the sweeping panoramic views from the top are appealing rewards. But when we give it our best and still do not make it – when we fail – the disappointment can be crushing.

Once my family and I were all safely descended and together again, we found a gorgeous place to stop for refreshments. I personally believe all the best walks end with a teashop, and this was a beauty: a cosy little place perched next to a stunning waterfall, where the friendly staff served us some of the best homemade brownies I have ever tried. Utter bliss! But as we sat and recovered from the exertion of the climb, even the scenery and the cake could not soothe my disappointment and so, wanting to protect my family's good mood from my sense of frustration, I took myself off for a solitary wander round the beautiful grounds. Not really concentrating on where I was going, I found myself following a winding path leading downhill. The air grew still, and the whispers of a rippling river echoed between steep wooded slopes on either side. There were no others around: the solitude was a relief from the felt pressure to support everyone else's needs. Here I did not have to keep pushing myself to be strong and to suppress my emotions. I could just breathe and be whatever I needed to be – disappointed, sad, frustrated. I stopped trying to force myself to cheer up and conceded my overwhelming sense of defeat.

The path ahead of me turned a corner, and as I came around the bend, I noticed a mossy stone plaque in the craggy wall at my side. Intrigued, I leaned in to read the inscription, written in beautiful Celtic lettering:

> *You must come away to some lonely place all by yourselves and rest for a while.*

I gasped aloud. It was as if God Himself had inscribed a personalised message to me and left it in the most perfect location for me to find just as I stopped striving. Here in this low, isolated valley – the very opposite of the exhilarating peak I had tried to reach – He was inviting me to rest with Him. He was not judging me on success or failure – just inviting me to be with Him where I was. The success of finishing that single journey was not the only reward available to me: HE is always our ultimate destination, and no physical limitation can ever keep us from Him. Peace filled my heart as the Holy Spirit took the words from that slab of moss-covered rock and breathed them into my heart to settle there.

I looked up the quote at home later that night and found it in Mark 6:31. I discovered that when Jesus originally spoke those words, He was talking to His disciples after a busy and intense season. His cousin John the Baptist had been beheaded by the Jewish king, Herod Antipas – martyred for daring to call the royal family to repentance. No doubt Jesus and His followers were in shock and grieving. And the disciples had just come back from a season of travelling ministry. Sent out in pairs, they had been travelling the towns and cities of Israel preaching the gospel and performing signs and wonders in Jesus' Name, in obedience to Jesus' commission.[11] It all sounds glamorous and exciting, but there would have been hardships too: Jesus did not go with them; they weren't allowed to take food, clothing, or money with them; these inexperienced men were really 'thrown in at the deep end' of learning to minister. No doubt it would have been thrilling, but still – exhausting. And, as they returned and told Jesus all they had done, His response to them was an invitation to come aside with Him to a deserted place – a wilderness – and to rest a while.

Ministry – by which I mean anything we *do* for God, whether it be prayer, preaching, serving, and so on – is a bit like climbing a mountain: it can be addictive. Especially when it is going well, and we feel 'I cannot stop now; there's too much ahead', or 'I need to keep encouraging the others'. And even when it is *not* going well, we can also feel driven to try harder, to push through until we reach our goal, because isn't quitting failure? But for God, the success or failure of our efforts is never His final purpose for us. Yes, ministry is an adventure, a co-labouring that He loves to share with us, His friends. But His ultimate goal for us is always relationship with Him. And when ministry takes over our focus, He often interrupts with an invitation

---

[11] Mark 6:7-13

to rest – to come away with Him to a place where there is nothing to do, so that we can remember the blessing of just being with Him, receiving His love and enjoying His presence. It's not failure, it's a gift. It just might not feel like it to our driven selves, but that shows why we need it so much.

In retrospect, that day was a turning point for me that marked the start of my current 'wilderness'. My descent from previous mountain-top experiences into a deep valley was a foreshadowing of how my life soon afterwards became hidden and difficult, no longer bearing obvious fruit, and how I became frustrated, knowing God had promised to be with me but still feeling trapped and unable to achieve anything I used to value, or to see where I was going. Rest is meant to be a blessing, but when you are used to busy abundant life and fruitfulness it can also be unwelcome and feel like failure.

Thankfully I have a single promise from God to cling to, from our opening verse – that this season has divine purpose, for me to come aside and be with Him. So, even though it has still been intensely hard as dry seasons always are, I am encouraged that He will eventually bring me through. And I wanted to share that hope with you too, right from the start of this journey. He hasn't left us alone, even if it feels like it – we're just learning to walk somewhere new and at a different pace, to find different treasures, and to remember that whatever we do – or don't do – *for* Him, it is always far less important in His eyes than simply being *with* Him. He isn't judging or disapproving of us but wanting to bless us with rest, so we can be restored to the simple enjoyment of being together. Nothing else needed.

So, today He calls us to stop striving, and says, 'Come away, My love, and rest with Me.'[12]

---

[12] Mark 6:31; Song of Songs 2:10

Chapter 3 – Place of WEEPING

"Blessed are those whose strength is in you,
whose hearts are set on pilgrimage.
As they pass through the Valley of Baka,
they make it a place of springs;
the autumn rains also cover it with pools.
They go from strength to strength,
till each appears before God in Zion."
Psalm 84:5-7

THE 'VALLEY OF Baka' mentioned in Psalm 84 translates as *Valley of Weeping*. Nobody seems to agree on exactly where this valley is, or how it got its name, but scholars mostly agree it was a known wilderness area – as was much of historic Israel.

Weeping seems to me to be a deep expression of emotional heartache, frustration, loneliness, or loss. It expresses the utmost internal pain that can be so often associated with difficult seasons, the peak of our sorrow when all rational reasoning is gone and our hurting overflows in tears. In one way I find it amazing that God created our physical bodies with the ability to handle intense emotional pain in this way, to be able to release the pressure of anguish when it becomes overwhelming. It is well known that suppressing tears can lead to mental or physical ill-health such as depression or hypertension, so we know that letting tears flow is healthy. Even so, it does not feel good at the time. We cry because we hurt. Weeping is the overflow of unbearable pain that we would give anything to escape.

How beautiful, then, that God is so intimately involved in those times. He does not just give us a way to release our sadness, but keeps it for us, like a priceless treasure not to be wasted. Psalm 56:8 tells us, "You keep track of all my sorrows. You have collected all my tears in your bottle. You have recorded each one in your book." (NLT)

Imagine that: Father God knows us so well, and is so attuned to our well-being, that He tracks our sorrows and collects our tears, recording them all as a loving parent who hears the crying of their child and rushes to give comfort every single time it is needed. When we weep, He is there – carefully and lovingly collecting each drop in order that they not be overlooked or unvalued. Our tears become like liquid prayers: carriers of our pain that is too deep to express in words. And God gathers our tears just as He receives our prayers, that He might answer and heal our pain.

Very often we can be blinded by tears, when physically our vision is blurred by the salt water in our eyes, but emotionally and spiritually they can stop us seeing God clearly too. I am thinking of the many psalms that start with pain and struggle – David and the other psalmists often could not see God through their agony to begin with either. But still as they poured out their pain with tears and cries, His patient love gently restored their souls, and He came back into their focus. It is what gives us hope in painful wilderness seasons: He will not leave us to suffer here forever. Weeping may endure for the night, but joy always comes in the morning – eventually.[13]

The most intense sorrow of my life was when I suffered each of my two miscarriages. Those who have read *Friend of God* will know the stories; I grieved hard and deep. It had taken so long for us to break free of barrenness with all that associated pain and grief, my heart as a new mother was very tender. So, when my second and fourth pregnancies ended with losing my babies before I could even hold them, taking my grief to God was not a glowing and glorious time of

---

[13] Psalm 30:5

communing with God. It was messy and raw – my heart felt like it was breaking wide open. To begin with I was not even conscious of His presence. All I knew was the pain I was immersed in: tears that soaked my pillow many nights, the cry of 'why?' that arose from the depths of my shattered soul, the unbearable ache in my arms to hold the babies that had been taken from me, the feeling that I was destroyed and would never recover. But as I wept, I knew that I had a choice: to turn my back on God in anger for allowing this to happen – or to turn *to* Him because He was the only One who could get me through. Don't get me wrong: I *was* angry – it is a normal stage of grieving, after all – and I did at times complain to and shout at Him. And yet, just like the psalmists of the Bible who so often did the same, at those times I would discover the truth that when the tempest passes, He is still there, still loving. He would absorb the pain manifesting as anger, hopelessness, and sorrow, and bring me through to the calm that follows a storm.

Over time I came to realise that as I walked through this dreadful valley of the shadow of death, He truly was with me.[14] And the blessing and restoration that came through that season was one of my life's most valued treasures. I don't know if I would ever have learned the truth and depth of His love had I not experienced that season of discovering His loving presence through the darkest night.

God catches our tears and turns them into pools of blessing. When I woke this morning and prepared to write this chapter, He showed me a picture – a sudden mental image of a dusty red wilderness valley, dry and rocky with very few parched-looking scrubby plants. Little pools were dotted about, reflecting rainbow colours though the sky was pale grey. I felt the Holy Spirit say, 'This is how I redeem your tears,' and He reminded me of my journey to survive miscarriage, and the verses from Psalm 84 we opened the chapter with.

Because in ourselves we can't make life-giving springs come out of our deepest sorrow. But God can. He does it when we walk with Him – He is the one who transforms and redeems. In this life on earth, we

---

14 Psalm 23:4

all have seasons of going through wilderness valleys: dry, lonely, and deeply painful places of weeping. But our tears are never wasted. God walks with us every step of the way, and as our tears make symbolic pools of water on the ground, He notices, records, honours, and redeems them with His promise (symbolised by the rainbow reflections in the picture He gave me). Our weeping is counted, treasured, and in Him is redeemed into something beautiful, so when we look back on our time in the valley, we too will see those pools reflecting His promise to be with us.

So, if you are in a valley of weeping right now, I pray that you will begin to know how closely God is walking with you, collecting every single tear; that the God who wept[15] has nothing but compassion for your pain, and plans to turn it into something beautiful. And that in time you too will see how He was with you every step of the way. Even if you cannot see Him through your tears just now, I pray you will.

---

[15] John 11:35

Chapter 4 – Place of LEARNING TO DEPEND ON JESUS

"Who is this coming up from the wilderness leaning
on her beloved?"
Song of Songs 8:5

I HAVE NOTICED a pattern over these past few wilderness years. Every year in the week between Christmas and the New Year, I seem to find myself reflecting over the year that has been, acknowledging the pain and loss experienced there, admitting that my desires for the year were not met as I hoped, though thankful to God for bringing me through. And I find myself looking to the approaching year, wondering if it will finally be the year that we receive the promised breakthrough.

At the end of 2021 I wrote in my journal, 'Lord, please help? I don't know if we can withstand this much relentless, ever-increasing pressure. I know there are many who are worse-off than us, and I know – truly – that as long as we have You, we have all we need. But I am still struggling, Lord – the pressure is relentless, and I feel so weak.'

As I re-read these words in late 2023, I wryly acknowledged that the sentiment remained the same. Two whole years later, and I was still feeling weak under the pressure of our circumstances. So, I read on, to see how God had answered my prayer the first time…

He had replied by reminding me of Martha and Mary in Luke 10:38-42 and then saying to me, *'My love, you are worried and upset about many things, but few things are needed – or indeed only one. Come, choose what is better and it will not be taken away from you. Come, sit at My feet and listen to Me.'*

There is a simple truth to be found in the wilderness. When we come to a place of hardship and pressure, where we must acknowledge that all *our* gifts and strengths are just not enough, that is where we truly learn to lean on Jesus. There we find that only He is fully enough.

In the past couple of weeks, I have been talking to Him about feeling overwhelmed. In truth I am NOT overwhelmed – His promise is the same today as it was when He spoke the words written in Isaiah 43:2 – "When you pass through the waters I will be with you; and through the rivers, they shall not overwhelm you." (RSV)

And yet the feeling of being overwhelmed – drowning in difficulty and unable to cope – persisted. So, I did the only thing I know to do, and spoke to God about it. As I prayed, I suddenly saw with my mind's eye a picture of someone treading water. I remembered a swimming lesson I had as a child where we were taught to tread water – if we ever fell into water we should kick off our shoes, remove heavy coats if possible, and then in a vertical position continually kick our feet and scull our arms to keep our heads above water. The goal was to practise until we could do this for long periods of time.

'That's interesting,' I mused aloud to God, 'nowadays they seem to teach children to do the starfish float instead.' (Again, this involves removing shoes and heavy coats if possible, but instead of assuming a vertical position, learning to float horizontally on their backs with arms and legs outstretched.) Still thinking out loud, I said, 'I guess that's because treading water is exhausting and can't be maintained for long periods, but floating conserves energy?'

'Exactly My point,' God said kindly. Right then, I realised He was telling me that in this season I had been trying to tread water in my own strength rather than just lying back in Him and waiting patiently for Him to come and rescue me, as He always does. That in seasons of overwhelming circumstances, trying to save ourselves by our own efforts – 'I must pray harder; I must think more positively; I must keep

going; I must… (insert your own efforts here)' – is pointless and exhausting. The best thing to do is lean back and 'float': accept we are in difficult circumstances, and accept we are unable to do anything except wait for Him and trust that He is on His way. It's a stance that says 'be still and know that He is God',[16] trusting that He is with us (even when we cannot see or feel Him) and that He is able to save us.[17] Depending on Jesus is like doing a starfish float when we are overwhelmed: we have no power to save ourselves, so lean back and wait for the One who runs to our rescue.[18]

There are a few reasons why people still try to tread water instead of adopting the laid-back starfish float, but the one that really stands out to me is that in treading water their panic has deceived them into thinking effort equals control. I realised this was the reason God had been repeatedly telling me throughout the wilderness season to keep my eyes fixed on Jesus.[19]

Seasons of overwhelming circumstances come to us all. If all we see is those circumstances, we will panic and potentially wear ourselves out trying to keep our heads above water in our own strength. But if we can learn to make a better choice: to tip our heads back to gaze upwards to Him and rest – inactive and floating on our backs, facing Him with arms and legs outstretched – trusting that He will never let us drown, we will be in a better position to survive. It is not a passive stance, but a deliberate act of letting go of striving and choosing to lie back, trusting that He is on His way. Because He is.

It's like the rest we talked about in Chapter 2, but with an extra dimension. Learning to depend on Jesus is all about trust: trusting that He sees us and trusting Him to rescue us, rather than wasting energy trying to save ourselves. The circumstances remain the same either way: scary, painful, and potentially overwhelming. God is not only bigger, but He is also faithful to keep His promises and mighty to save. We can trust Him.

---

[16] Psalm 46:10
[17] Zephaniah 3:17
[18] Psalm 70:1
[19] Hebrews 12:2

So, if you are feeling overwhelmed today – whether by difficult circumstances, emotional or physical pain and exhaustion, or the mental demands of a non-stop busy season, or any other reason, I pray that you won't try to solve it yourself or keep striving in desperation. Rather that you will acknowledge the reality of your situation and simply look to God, who loves to save you. Lean back and know He has got you – He won't let you down! And I pray you will hear His voice calling to you as He has also been calling to me: *'Remember to starfish float! I will not let you drown in it all – I am on my way!'* AMEN!

Chapter 5 – Place of WRESTLING

*"That night Jacob got up and took his two wives, his two
female servants and his eleven sons and crossed the ford of the
Jabbok. After he had sent them across the stream, he sent over
all his possessions. So Jacob was left alone, and a man wrestled
with him till daybreak."*
Genesis 32:22-24

Jacob and his family were in the wilderness, in the middle of a great journey across hostile desert lands. After Jacob sent his family and possessions across the Jabbok ford, he was left all alone in the darkest point of night – the epitome of so many wilderness experiences: dark, lonely, terrifying, and painful.

There is so much about Jacob that fascinates me. Despite a deceitful start, he would become the third of the three Hebrew patriarchs. Abraham was the first: father of faith and friend of God. Isaac was the second: forerunner of Christ, the obedient son who willingly laid down his life. But it was Jacob – the cheat who deceived his father and tricked his brother out of birthright and blessing, and who wrestled painfully with God – who saw the fulfilment of God's promise and personally fathered the twelve tribes of God's chosen nation. And it was Jacob whose name was so often associated with God's, as in the case of 'God of Jacob' throughout the Bible.[20]

---

[20] e.g. Psalm 24:6

What I love most about Jacob is that he never let go. He embraced the struggle of our humanity. His mistakes and flaws are written out for all to see. But he still had the audacity to hang onto God and refuse to let go until he received the blessing he knew he could not do without. Moses may have seen God face to face, and Elijah may have had the faith to defeat the enemy in a dramatic showdown, but it was gloriously human, broken Jacob who in the middle of his wilderness grabbed hold of God and refused to let go, no matter the cost. He could not even see who he was wrestling in the middle of the night. The Bible says it was 'a man', whom some identify as an angel, while others recognise this as a Christophany – Jesus appearing in the flesh before He was born a human – but regardless, Jacob clung to God's agent and would not let go until dawn broke and he could see who he was wrestling. Did he know who he was fighting with? Possibly not to start with – it is unclear. All we know is that at some point Jacob obviously realised, because by daybreak, when the man asked to be released, Jacob then demanded the blessing, and after he received it, said, "I saw God face to face, and yet my life was spared."[21]

We all come to wilderness seasons in our lives when we struggle, often not even knowing who we are fighting with: is it an attack of the enemy trying to defeat us? Are we struggling with our own human habits, like Paul?[22] Or is God Himself holding us back, like with Jacob? Not knowing can be the hardest part of the fight. And the thought of God actively fighting with us seems terrifying: we are so weak and finite compared to Him, He could obliterate us without moving. But Jesus is our intercessor, standing between us and God's punishment, so why *would* God fight us?

As I was writing this chapter I remembered how my three sons used to love play-fighting with Daddy. They would throw themselves wholeheartedly into the wrestle, and although I was often concerned that somebody might get injured, they never did. Because the thing is, although Daddy was bigger and stronger than them, he was not

---

[21] Genesis 32:30
[22] Romans 7:15 NLT

fighting to hurt them. He was not even fighting to win. He was wrestling to engage with them, both to have fun playing and to help them discover their limits. As I was writing this chapter I asked my husband for his take on it, and he said something I find fascinating. He said that helping children discover the limits of their power is not a negative thing, as some might imagine, but positive: it helps them realise they are more powerful than they imagined, and they learn the areas they need to develop in.

Now apply that to God, wrestling with Jacob in the wilderness. Jacob had just escaped a run-in with Laban, his uncle who had mistreated him for decades, and was on his way to meet Esau, his brother who had vowed to kill him. This was a man who knew he needed God – that he could not make it on his own. So, God met him and wrestled with him, until he learned his limitations – his strengths and weaknesses – and learned who he was: no longer Jacob, but Israel, founder of God's chosen nation. He may have been left with a limp – a visible sign of his human weakness – but now he also knew he was a man with God's blessing.

So, let's consider our own seasons of wrestling in that light: the times when it feels like we are engaging with resistance from God. In the push and pull and struggle of it all, what if God isn't fighting us because He's against us, but because He's on our side, like the best dad ever wanting to help us discover our strengths and our limits, wanting to enjoy the connection of engaging even when it's not comfortable?

Because wrestling *is* uncomfortable, challenging work that can be painful – it demands intense focus and effort that does not allow for any distraction. But then, walking with God is not easy. I don't know why we imagine it would be, when Jesus Himself said, "In this world you will have trouble."[23] We tend to think that if we were following Jesus in every area, all would be well, and we would be surrounded by blessing. But while it's true that God loves to bless us, a trouble-free life here on Earth just isn't biblical. Some blessings only come when we have to wrestle things through, and that's not a sign of failure, it's our

---

[23] John 16:33

opportunity to grab hold and hang on, in a way that makes us better appreciate the value of what we need the most. It is single-minded pursuit of the prize.

Unlike the playtimes my boys used to enjoy with their daddy, one of the most difficult things for us about wrestling with God in the wilderness is that like Jacob, we rarely see what is going on or who we are wrestling with until it's over and daylight breaks. We do not know if God is against us or if we are fighting an enemy out to destroy us. But I am convinced that either way, if we hang onto God through the darkness when we cannot see what is going on, eventually dawn will break and we will receive clarity. We will find God in it, and we will receive the blessing He delights to give us in return.

Friends and fellow wilderness-travellers, I know the wrestling can be exhausting, but we can take heart: morning is coming, and God will reveal Himself to us in it if we do not let go. And, like Jacob, we will never be the same again.

Chapter 6 – Place of REVIVAL

"The hand of the Lord was on me, and he brought me out by the Spirit of the Lord and set me in the middle of a valley; it was full of bones. He led me back and forth among them, and I saw a great many bones on the floor of the valley, bones that were very dry."
Ezekiel 37:1-2

THROUGHOUT MY CURRENT wilderness season, I have been getting up early to meet with God, as is my habit. I freely acknowledge that it's much harder to do so in dry times than in times when I'm experiencing the flow of the Holy Spirit infusing me with energy to get up and get going. I have been doing it out of habit, discipline, and a stubborn clinging to God's promise to be with me even when I cannot *feel* His presence. But I admit there have also been seasons in my life when I stopped altogether, so if that's where you are, don't feel condemned: there is still hope.

The dryness of the wilderness can feel like it has sapped every bit of life and energy, leaving us as dusty, shrivelled up versions of those we once thought we were. As we travel through our desert season, there are occasional pools of refreshing along the way: places where we feel lifted with a dose of grace that helps to keep us going to the next oasis. But still, the longer we are there the more we are tempted to feel completely dried up like a pile of old bones: present (just), but as dusty and lifeless as our environment.

How beautiful then that the Bible contains this exact picture in Ezekiel 37. As I came to pray this morning, hoping that today might be a beautiful oasis day but wanting to worship God by turning up even if I felt nothing, I sensed a kind of inner prompt telling me God was waiting to show me something. It took me a while to tune in – I have been feeling out of practice – but what He said was deeply encouraging. He spoke words of blessing and restoration, giving me hope that my wilderness time will be ending soon. And He took me to Ezekiel 37, to the barren valley of scattered dry bones, and His question to the prophet there, "Can these bones live?"[24]

I felt like God was with me, looking at my life through my eyes, seeing it as a mere skeleton of the spiritual life I used to have – all life and flesh stripped away, with nothing left but disjointed and scattered bones. And as I read through the chapter and echoed Ezekiel's words, "Lord, only you know,"[25] I felt fresh hope begin to stir at the mere possibility that even when a situation looks finished, God still sees the chance for a new beginning…

I love this chapter's heading, because I doubt many people associate the word 'revival' with the wilderness. When people speak of revival, they usually think of God doing an exciting and sovereign work to reveal Himself to large crowds of people. And yes, those are great. There are some who have studied past revivals and think they have found the key to unlocking another one in our times; this usually revolves around praying more, fasting more, and being more devoted. Those things are also great. But as I read Ezekiel 37 this morning, I suddenly realised there is one main thing that qualifies something for revival more than anything else: it must be dead!

For something to be re-vived, first it must be 'un-vived'. It is a sobering thought for those trying to be holy enough/persistent enough in prayer: perhaps we just need to acknowledge our dead-as-dry-bones status and cry out for God in His mercy to do a miracle and bring us back to life.

---

[24] Ezekiel 37:3
[25] Ezekiel 37:3

So, for those of us in the valley of dry bones, feeling like all life and order is a distant memory, the revival in Ezekiel 37 gives us hope of a true, miraculous, resurrection revival – the kind of revival we need in our personal lives. And as I read it this morning, I was encouraged by the process.

First God asked Ezekiel if the bones could live. Faced with a dry and scattered collection of long-dead remains, Ezekiel said the only wise thing he could: "You alone know." When we are in that kind of hope-long-gone place and we look through human eyes, it does not seem possible that anything could come of our life now: we feel immersed in the endless dryness of it all. But in God's eyes nothing is impossible. And, regardless of our feelings, it is always wise to remember He is greater.

So, God asked Ezekiel to prophesy to the bones: to speak out words that contradicted what he was seeing and feeling, and to command them to live, on behalf of God. God's promises, like the one spoken to and through Ezekiel here, always bring new life and new hope. And there is power when we speak them out loud. God could have spoken to the piles of bones Himself, but He didn't. He got Ezekiel involved; He asked him to speak with authority. And based on the promise he had just received, Ezekiel did just that.[26]

First, he commanded the bones to come together, working with what was already there. Next, he called the tendons, flesh, and skin to grow back, which required a creative miracle. Then he spoke the breath of God into them, repeating the process of creation when God made Adam,[27] and reminding us that even if something looks whole, true life is impossible without the Holy Spirit whose very name, *Ruach,* means 'breath'. Each step reminds us that much as we would like an instant deliverance from our dry and dead state, sometimes God revives us in stages, each one building on the faith developed in the previous stage. So, if we're not seeing instant answer to prayer yet, we can still have hope in God's process.

---

[26] Ezekiel 37:4-10
[27] Genesis 2:7

And it didn't stop there – in an important fourth stage, the revived beings STOOD and took their place in the army.[28] Standing up demonstrates autonomy – it can only be done by living beings revived to determine their own action. When they took their place in an army it showed that revival does not just return us to the status quo: we are revived to fresh purpose, fresh equipping.

If you are still in the wilderness and all this sounds too far from where you are at – lovely for someone else, but you cannot relate – that's no problem. I don't want you to feel you are lacking or failing by not being here just yet. I just want to let you know that it is coming. Your current dried-up state and feelings are utterly discouraging, I know. It feels like you cannot see the end or the way out. But God can. He is not going to leave you there – He has a plan to revive you and bring you out, as miraculously as turning an old heap of scattered bones into a living, breathing army.

---

[28] Ezekiel 37:10

Chapter 7 – Place where GOD HIDES

"You, God, are my God, earnestly I seek you. I thirst for you,
my whole being longs for you, in a dry and parched land
where there is no water."

Psalm 63:1

ONE OF THE most distressing hallmarks of wilderness seasons, which can feel most acute the first time we find ourselves there, is the sense that God has withdrawn. Remember Jesus' cry on the cross: "My God, my God, why have you abandoned me?"[29] For a child of God, the worst pain in the world is to feel separated from Him. We know that in God's Word He promises He will always be with us.[30] So, in seasons when it *feels* like God has left us and gone into hiding, it can be confusing and upsetting. As David said in Psalm 30:7, "When You hid Your face, I was dismayed."

For some, when we become Christians, that first period of seeing Him is filled with the warm glow of first love: our eyes are instantly opened to how kind, forgiving and loving He is; His deep eternal love fills our hearts and assures us we truly belong to Him; in finding Him we have satisfied the deep need in our lives, and we never want to let go. Others find Jesus more gradually and do not experience this 'falling in love' as instantly but get to know Him better over time: prayer may begin simply and clumsily, but we trust He is listening and little by

---

[29] Matthew 27:46 NLT
[30] Matthew 28:20

little we learn to recognise His voice. The Bible gradually makes more sense and comes to feel more alive than before. We grow into loving relationship with God more slowly, but just as surely.

But however we start, inevitably a day comes to all Christians when we realise that lovely warm sense of His loving presence is missing. We don't feel so connected as we once did. Prayer seems like a ritual; we are uncertain if He is listening. If we read the Bible, it is out of duty, but it does not feel as alive as it did. And other Christians start to irritate us with their flaws. We feel dry and empty, like lonely wanderers in a strange and barren land. We ask ourselves where God went and what we did wrong to end up alone in this arid, dusty place. How will we survive without Him? Will we ever find Him again, or have we lost our way for good?

But the wilderness is not the punishment we think: it is a place where God takes His beloved to develop deeper intimacy. It is a holy place where we learn to seek and find Him.

While I was writing this chapter, I felt God showed me an analogy of a child who had been adopted into a family. This child had never known the love of a father and had missed out on many experiences. When they first played hide and seek with their new dad, they were terrified when he disappeared. The other children who had grown up in that family weren't scared: from their baby years Daddy had played 'peek-a-boo' with them, hiding his face behind his hands for a few seconds and then moving his hands away to make eye contact again, instilling the trust in them from a very early age that he is always present and always comes back into view. But the newly adopted child, familiar with isolation and abandonment, felt the sense of loss keenly and feared they had done something wrong that meant he was gone forever – that they were alone again.

It seems to me that this is like some of us as Christians the very first time we experience God seeming to withdraw: we blame ourselves and fear we have lost God's presence for good. It is a scary place to be, and like David in Psalm 63, our sense of loss is all the keener because now we have known what it is like to feel close to God.

And I believe that is the point. Because when I pictured the imaginary adopted child finding their dad again, their thankfulness was all the greater, and the fears that had previously been hidden but had now come to the surface could be dealt with as their father drew them close and whispered, 'Remember my promise: I will never leave you.'[31] God hides from us temporarily and allows us to feel the full force of how much we miss and long for Him, so that He can bless us with an even greater measure of His presence as we seek Him wholeheartedly. And just so we can be sure He wants to be found, He put multiple promises in the Bible…

- "Draw near to God and He will draw near to you." (James 4:8 NKJV)

- "You will seek me and find me when you seek me with all your heart." (Jeremiah 29:13)

- "I love those who love me, and those who seek me find me." (Proverbs 8:17)

- "Seek the Lord while he may be found; call on him while he is near." (Isaiah 55:6)

- "Seek the Lord your God, you will find Him if you seek Him with all your heart and with all your soul." (Deuteronomy 4:29)

- "Seek and you will find." (Matthew 7:7)

So, if you are feeling today like God has withdrawn and left you alone, please be encouraged: He hasn't gone for good; He's just calling, *'Come and look for Me – I want to be found by you!'*

---

[31] Deuteronomy 31:8; Hebrews 13:5

Chapter 8 – Place of
AUTHENTIC PRAYER

"Jesus often withdrew to the wilderness for prayer."
Luke 5:16 (NLT)

I HESITATED WHEN naming this chapter: when we are in a dry wilderness season, prayer can feel like the last thing we are able to do! We know we desperately need God and that we *should* pray, but any prayers we do force out feel like they are just bouncing off the ceiling. After all, in the loneliest seasons where we have lost the experience of God's presence, what reason do we have to believe that anyone, let alone God, is listening to our words? And, conscious of those readers who are struggling right now, I did not want the heading to cause anyone to avoid this chapter, thinking it is going to be another recitation of the things we *should* be doing. Because the truth is, God's compassion is so much bigger than the religious 'shoulds' we pick up along the way. He knows us and understands all our human frailties and temptations because Jesus went through it all Himself. So, we know we have a Saviour who is not judging us but is with us in it all, offering grace and help, not judgement of our failure![32]

However, unable to think of a heading that would accurately reflect this truth that has become one of my favourite aspects of the wilderness, I am sticking with prayer as a title, because ultimately I believe it is one of the main reasons God takes us all through these

---

[32] Hebrews 4:15-16

seasons: because He wants us to learn the truth that Jesus knew – that authentic prayer is not a demanding duty to fail at, but the biggest blessing of all. For it is here, far from human influence and distraction, that we are most free to abandon the emptiness of religious jargon and simply talk to God. It is here that we have the best opportunity to deepen our relationship with Him through conversation. Here is where He wants to be found, not as a demander of religious duties but as a father who loves us.

For Jesus, prayer was not a chore or a duty, nor a spiritual discipline He had to commit to if He wanted to be more anointed. It was a treasured place to get one-to-one undisturbed time with God. Prayer was His rest, refreshment and restoration – a place of perfect completeness that could only be found when alone with God. So, when we are feeling dry, exhausted, and unable to pray, how can we possibly find God through prayer? What did Jesus know about prayer that we do not?

There is a clue in the opening two words of the Lord's Prayer:[33] "Our Father." Up until Jesus' ministry began, Jews had prayed to God in deference as their Creator and Lord for thousands of years. Nobody had ever dared to presume the kind of intimate familial relationship encapsulated by the name 'Father'. Nowadays, two thousand years of Christian culture later, the impact of that single noun is lost on us. But at the time it must have been utterly shocking and radical. Jesus had spoken of *His* Father – and indeed, God had endorsed Jesus as His Son at His baptism – but now Jesus was making it clear that we are *all* God's children… He said, "OUR Father." And, in teaching us how to pray to God as our dad, He showed us the absolute priority of prayer: not to come bowing and scraping to some dominant power, but to approach Him in relationship. Yes, with the respect He deserves, but also with intimacy and the certain knowledge that we are beloved children.[34]

---

[33] Matthew 6:9-13
[34] 1 John 3:2

There is another big clue in the word translated as 'prayer' in Matthew 6, as well as in this chapter's opening verse. It is the Greek word *proseuchomai*. It's a blend of two words: *pros* (meaning towards, or exchange) and *euxomai* (meaning to wish, or pray). Used together in this way, the true meaning of prayer carries a sense of exchanging wishes. It refers to us bringing our wishes and desires and needs to God, giving them to Him that we might receive the faith to meet our needs – *and* to listen to Him and receive His desires. It is a two-way conversation between those in a two-way relationship.

When Jesus went to the wilderness to pray, I do not believe He was just carrying a list of pleas and demands for His Father to provide for, waiting for God to say 'yes' or 'no' and then to move on accordingly. I am sure there was an element of needs and requests, but authentic prayer as a conversation is so much more besides. He would have gone to listen, to hear encouragement from His Father, to be refreshed by being in His company, to be reminded of God's heart, not just for Him, but for the people He was sent to. To exchange wishes and concerns; to give and receive love.

Nobody knows exactly what Jesus prayed when He was alone – it was not recorded. But I think it naïve to imagine He never had to pour out His own frustration, exhaustion and/or cries for help. None of those are sinful, but all are very human – as He was. And what He discovered – during the forty-day fast at the start of His ministry, as well as every wilderness session afterwards – was that when we are prepared to go through discomfort and deprivation in order to seek our Father, He will always meet us there to restore, refresh, and strengthen us for what is to come.

THAT is authentic prayer. And so, our feeble little whispers for help that feel like nobody is listening are an entirely valid expression of prayer. When we are in those desperate desert seasons, our prayers are rarely well formulated petitions. Sometimes we clumsily pour out our sorrows and complaints as David did in many psalms. Sometimes we have no words but can only weep (remember the liquid prayers of our tears in Chapter 3?) or experience groans deep in our soul that the

Holy Spirit carries straight to God without words.[35] Sometimes all we can do is cry out 'help!' And sometimes when we listen, we hear nothing in response, but still the Holy Spirit moves to comfort our souls.

Because however pitiful the prayer in our own eyes, Father God loves honest, authentic communication from our heart, far more than He does a cleverly worded speech. He loves us to come as children, and He loves to respond. He is not waiting for us to speak prayers that are so perfect they guarantee the answer we desire. If it was all about making our prayers flawless enough to release the answer, we wouldn't need Him: prayer would be a formula. But it's not – it is conversation, with our Heavenly Dad.

Sometimes I think the wilderness exists to teach us there ARE no perfect prayers. He does not want us to pray just so He can dispense the answer, like a divine vending machine. He wants us to pray because He wants us to talk to Him – to get to know Him in relationship as our Father, our Bridegroom, our Friend. And when we reach the point where we realise the answers are not the answer, but HE is the answer, that is when we have learned what the wilderness has to teach us about prayer.

---

[35] Romans 8:26

Chapter 9 – Place of DEPRIVATION

"Then Jesus was led by the Spirit into the wilderness to be
tempted by the devil.
After fasting forty days and forty nights, he was hungry."
Matthew 4:1-2

T HIS IS OUR second look at the passage above, because I believe
there is more treasure to be found here. At the time of writing,
I am fasting through Lent. I've never paid much attention to
Lent before – I knew it was a church tradition, but I wasn't sure of its
relevance. But when I felt led to write a devotional for this season, I
investigated it. I discovered that although Lent is not specifically
mentioned in the Bible, the tradition is based on the forty days that
Jesus spent in the wilderness fasting from all food and being tempted
by the enemy to serve His own needs and desires. Those who observe
Lent do so hoping to grow closer to Jesus by honouring the season of
deprivation that He experienced.

When I learned that, I knew it was going to be relevant to writing
this book. And as I approached Lent this year, I felt led to join in – not
just because it is a religious tradition, but because I identified with that
desire to be closer to Jesus. I also wanted to understand more of why
His period of self-denial was so important.

Scholars believe Jesus was about thirty years old when He began
His ministry. As Jews traditionally held adulthood to begin at around
thirteen years old, that means He had been living as an adult for

approximately seventeen years before His ministry began. What was going on during those silent years? The Bible does not tell us much, except that He was a carpenter (a master craftsman skilled with many materials, not just wood). And it appears that at some point His earthly father Joseph died. Perhaps Jesus took responsibility for His family until His younger siblings were old enough to financially care for Mary and the others? Maybe there were other reasons Jesus' ministry was not launched until His thirties. Whatever the reason, I find it most striking that He seems to have lived a devoted but otherwise 'normal' – dare I say comfortable? – human life, until His ministry began with two clear successive events:

First, His baptism. As we saw in Chapter 1, He did not need to repent or be cleansed of sin – He had none. It was a public symbolic expression of His 'new life' or ministry as One wholly identified with humankind and yielded to obeying God's purpose for His life. This was immediately followed by the second event: his fasting in the wilderness.

Jesus' baptism was a beautiful single moment of commitment and dedication, immediately followed by God's public approval: the kind of high point we all love. But we all know there is a world of difference between committing to something in a glorious moment and then persevering through the hardships and temptations that follow. So, Jesus' single moment of baptism in water was followed by forty days of fasting in the wilderness, learning the practical realities of daily denying Himself and submitting to God's will, and establishing the foundations for His ministry of total dependence on and devotion to God.

People talk about the devil tempting Jesus at the end of His fast as if that was the point of the whole forty-day period, but I don't think it was that simple. It wasn't just the enemy that Jesus overcame – it was also His own daily appetites, which can be harder to conquer than any external temptation. He learned to lean on God moment by moment, to discover the truth He would later declare: "My food is to do the will of him who sent me and to finish his work."[36] I believe it was this season of focused self-denial and voluntary deprivation as demonstrated through fasting where He really learned the strength He would need at Gethsemane when He was tempted again to serve His own needs, but overcame with, "Not my will, but Yours be done."[37]

There is something about fasting that exposes our most basic physical needs – our literal appetites, but not just that of our stomach. Deprivation exposes us emotionally. We see this expressed in the modern term 'hangry' that refers to the short-temperedness arising when our bodies need food. When we feel physically weak and tired our emotions are often harder to govern. Whether we feel irritable, hopeless, frustrated, or just less resilient than normal, we are typically more prone to react emotionally than when we are well nourished. We are weakened and more vulnerable to reacting from our physical flesh, rather than drawing on the Spirit of God within us.

Even when we are being deprived of something other than food – be it sleep, comfort, or relationships – deprivation leaves us weak and hungry on many levels, with all our appetites exposed and demanding to be met. And when our natural appetites are loudest, learning to deny them and turn to God in prayer helps us to walk in greater spiritual victory and authority.

So, the Holy Spirit led Jesus to this season of deprivation knowing it would leave Him physically and emotionally weak, needing to depend fully on God in order to overcome. And when Jesus was hungry, weak, and targeted by the enemy, the strength He found in God and the victory that He won became a beautiful foreshadowing of the ultimate victory He would win for us all at Gethsemane and the cross. For that was where He took deprivation and self-denial to its ultimate expression, voluntarily deprived of life itself and denying His own will to die for us.

Maybe you haven't chosen to fast throughout Lent. Maybe your season of deprivation has come in other areas – perhaps you have

---

[36] John 4:34
[37] Luke 22:42

moved away from friends or lost loved ones. Or maybe you are in a season where good health has been taken from you and you don't know if or when it will ever come back. When the blessings we take for granted are denied us, we become so much more appreciative when they return and quicker to recognise them in future. And in the meantime, we learn that even when our normal needs are not met, God is there: that in our weakness we can learn His strength.[38]

If you are experiencing deprivation today, I pray that God works through this season to give you comfort and strength, and to bless you with a deeper understanding of the victory won for us by Jesus, in His precious Name.

N.B. For more on the practice of fasting, see Appendix 2.

---

[38] 2 Corinthians 12:10

Chapter 10 – Place of DESTINY

"Throw him into this cistern here in the wilderness, but don't lay a hand on him."
Genesis 37:22

O F ALL THE stories of destiny in the Bible, surely that of Joseph (the eleventh son of Jacob) must be one of the most dramatic! Born to a barren woman and favoured by both parents, Joseph stood out as different from the start. By the time he became a teenager he was dreaming dreams that pointed even more to his future greatness. However, his ten brothers were not pleased for him. Taking sibling rivalry to an all-time low, they grew jealous and hate-filled and plotted together to murder him. Unknown to Joseph, his great destiny was about to be threatened at the age of just seventeen.

But God had a plan – a plan that would not just save him but his entire family and make them into a mighty nation. Biggest brother Reuben managed to talk down his murderous siblings to compromise. Rather than killing Joseph, he persuaded them to throw him into a cistern in the wilderness: a deep pit like a well with no water in it. Reuben planned to retrieve Joseph later and take him home after his brothers had cooled off, but God's bigger plan required more than a short overnight spell in the pit. Things were going to get much worse for Joseph, taking him from pit to slavery to prison, through a process that would last thirteen years.

Joseph's pit experience must have been a shock. From a lifestyle of relative comfort and pampering – his ornate robe a sign of the indulgence of his parents – he was now brutally stripped and thrown into a dark and dusty hole. The robe that had cloaked him with love and favour was taken away – he was betrayed, rejected, and alone. And it was only just beginning.

How many of us can relate? When we have our first wilderness experience it can feel like such a rude awakening. Suddenly we realise we have taken for granted the blessings around us; the comforts of family and/or friends, the daily provision that met all our needs, the felt presence and favour of our loving Father. Then suddenly we are plunged into painful, lonely darkness. Perhaps a loved one lets us down, or our path takes a very different turn away from the promises we believed God had been speaking over us. Confused, we ask ourselves what happened. How could our loved ones betray us? It is not fair... or is it? Did we somehow deserve it? And what about those promises? Did we hear wrong?

But much like Joseph, sometimes we find ourselves in the wilderness not because we did wrong or did not do right, but because God can see a bigger picture – because His plan to save us and those we love cannot be realised any other way. For after Joseph's pit led to thirteen years of slavery and imprisonment, there came a glorious and utterly overwhelming day when justice was served and he was not just set free, he was promoted to a position of immense authority second only to Pharaoh in importance. Now, Joseph was empowered to save Egypt and the surrounding nations (including his family) from a disastrous famine. And so, his teenage dreams of long ago had finally come true, in a way that could never have happened had he stayed in Canaan. And after another nine years, when finally reunited with his brothers, he told them, "But God sent me ahead of you to preserve for you a remnant on earth and to save your lives by a great deliverance. So then, it was not you who sent me here, but God."[39]

---

[39] Genesis 45:7-8

Sometimes when we fall into a wilderness pit (or end up in one thanks to somebody else's actions), we can feel completely let down by others, and God most of all. But sometimes the pit is the doorway to a difficult season that is going to result in breakthrough – not just for us, but for many others too. Maybe our current journey is such a season, which will result in breakthrough and freedom for more people than we can imagine. We might not be able to see it, just as Joseph would have had no idea about where his journey would take him. But just as Joseph must have trusted God, so we can learn the same.

From his time down the well, slavery, and imprisonment, as well as the favour and pit-to-palace promotion that followed, Joseph learned many valuable character traits: humility, wisdom, and thankfulness – and possibly most importantly, he learned that when we submit to God's leading and plan for our lives, He can work through us to perform outstanding miracles that affect so many more than just us.

In my own wilderness seasons I have found great comfort in Joseph's story. Sure, he made some unwise choices (boasting about his dreams of power to jealous siblings may not have been the wisest move), but he didn't deserve the harsh set of circumstances that followed. And yet, he did not become bitter and rail against God for allowing it but chose to humbly receive the path set before him, acting with integrity and honour every step of the way until God's timing for Joseph's reward and restoration was fulfilled.

When we find ourselves in a pit, suddenly far away from comfort, and perhaps even feeling abandoned by God, may we too learn the lessons Joseph learned. May we not let our hearts grow bitter with complaint and self-pity, but may we humble ourselves to keep our hearts tender towards Him and keep honouring Him in all we do. Then His rewards and restoration will also catch up with us, and we will see His goodness anew, when the wilderness season has accomplished what it was intended for.

Chapter 11 – Place of LONELINESS

"And he said to them, 'Come away by yourselves to a lonely place…'"
Mark 6:31 (RSV)

I KNOW WE have referred to this Bible verse before, but as God often takes me back to Bible passages to give fresh revelation each time, I figured it was OK for me to do the same!

When I posted a quick research question on social media, asking what three words people most associated with the word 'wilderness', the words that cropped up by far the most were 'lonely' and 'alone'. Loneliness seems to be one of the most unbearable elements of these seasons. For one of the first things God said to mankind at the beginning of Creation was, "It is not good for man to be alone."[40] Jesus' cry on the cross, "Why have You abandoned me?"[41] shows that He knows the immense pain of feeling alone. And that awareness may be the reason the last thing Jesus is recorded as saying to us in Matthew 28:20 was, "I am with you always, to the very end of the age." During this wilderness time of my own, I can confirm that one of the hardest, most painful things about this season is the sense of isolation here. It is at times unbearably lonely.

Now, I am married to a good man, have three wonderful children and a lovely extended family, and am blessed to know many friends. I

---

[40] Genesis 2:18
[41] Matthew 27:46 NLT

am not on my own in human terms. And yet that is no protection against loneliness. For there are always times when no other human being can satisfy the needs within us. There will always be times through life when people will hurt us and let us down. Nobody's perfect, and sadly imperfect people do hurt each other. And when we enter a wilderness place where our walk with God seems drier and harder, but we can't explain how, it can be difficult for people to know how to help. They may try to offer advice or comfort, but when we remain in a place of spiritual discomfort that is not easily fixed, they run out of ideas and eventually move on – very often to deal with their own troubles – so we, their struggling friends, can feel even more alone.

In my own loneliness I have at times reached out for help and found none. There have been times when I desperately needed a friend to pray with me, but people were simply too busy; and other times when there would have been people willing to pray, but I just didn't know how to express my need. There have even been times when people have offered to pray and then prayed prayers that left me feeling judged or written off and even more lonely than ever. I'm not seeking pity or to blame anyone – accusing others at times like this is irrelevant. The point is, if I ask even good people to meet a need that God wants to meet Himself, I will never be satisfied. Sometimes it is only when we are let down that we eventually turn to God, as He desires.

It is not that He wants us to be lonely, or even that He allows loneliness to draw us to Himself, though I think there is some truth in the latter. It's more that loneliness is a result of our trying to satisfy our need for Him through others. Inevitably they will always – eventually – fail, as nobody is able to be the perfect companion that God is. Some of our needs were never meant to be met by others, otherwise we might forget our need for Him. And the truth is, only He can truly satisfy us.

He doesn't want to be our last hope – He wants to be the One we turn to first. Because He is the only One who will never let us down. Whether friends, family, even spouses – no one is supposed to take precedence over Him in our affections or be our primary port of call in times of need. Loved ones are absolutely a blessing from Him, but we all go through seasons when friends or family cannot be there for us, for very good reason. And if we haven't learned by then that God is our first and very best friend, it can take a painful path of loneliness to learn that lesson.

Like the psalmist who said, "Turn to me and be gracious to me, for I am lonely and afflicted,"[42] we must cry out to God, for He has promised to never leave or forsake us.[43] And He is here. So, we must learn to keep crying to Him, to receive what we need the most from the Holy Spirit, our best Friend who truly sticks closer than a brother.[44] In times of the loneliest isolation, God Himself does not just want to give us a friend; He wants us to find HIM as the answer to our prayers for a dependable friend. And sometimes that's a lesson that can only be learned when all others truly have forsaken us. As painful as loneliness is, God will allow it as the kindest gift that leads us to find Him, the One who never leaves us alone.

---

[42] Psalm 25:16
[43] Deuteronomy 31:8
[44] Proverbs 18:24

Chapter 12 – Place where GOD SPEAKS

"The voice of the Lord shakes the desert."
Psalm 29:8

THIS CHAPTER BRINGS me to another of my favourite things about the wilderness. I can't say I ever enjoy these difficult times, but I have learned to value the blessings they contain. Of course, those seasons do not always start that way: when we first find ourselves here, we usually go through a period of adjusting to the new and difficult environment, questioning how we got here, where God has gone, and if we are going to survive. That first part is the most painful, and depending on how long we remain here, we may revisit those questions several times over. But eventually, if we keep seeking God through the hardships, we always find Him (see Chapter 7), because the beautiful truth is that God not only loves to hang out in the wilderness, but also this is where He loves to speak.

The Hebrew word for wilderness, *midbar,* can also be translated as 'mouth' or 'speech'. One word, two different but linked meanings. For it is where God loves to bring His people so He can speak to them.

We may feel like He is far away and has stopped speaking – that we cannot hear Him anymore. But our feelings, heightened by the difficulties of this place, are not the whole truth. If we seek and keep seeking, we *will* find Him and hear His word to us, because it is a promise.[45] And this promise is one that many biblical characters discovered to be true.

Think about Moses, hearing God's voice coming from the burning bush in the desert.[46] And later, with Israel in the wilderness: "As the sound of the trumpet grew louder and louder, Moses spoke and the voice of God answered him."[47]

Whoa! I think I am grateful God does not speak to me quite so dramatically. Even sometimes in the New Testament when God spoke to Jesus and Paul, it was thunderous, ground-shaking stuff![48]

But think about Elijah, who also heard God's voice on the mountain: "Then a great and powerful wind tore the mountains apart and shattered the rocks before the LORD, but the LORD was not in the wind. After the wind there was an earthquake, but the LORD was not in the earthquake. After the earthquake came a fire, but the LORD was not in the fire. And after the fire came a gentle whisper."[49]

God was in the whisper *after* the drama this time. And that seems more like the way we tend to hear God nowadays: so quiet we must lean in – especially in dry seasons! In the Old Testament, the prophets who heard God's voice usually did so externally, using their physical ears on the rare occurrences when He audibly spoke. For those of us in the New Covenant, we now have the Holy Spirit dwelling inside us. He speaks internally, in a still small voice we must learn to discern. In our day-to-day lives, there are many voices pressing in upon us: the voices of our own flesh, whether needs, wants, thoughts, or emotions; the voices of others, like family and friends who share their traditions or opinions; the voices of society's pressures and norms that may or may not be godly. Plus, there are temptations direct from the enemy too. And of course, if we have been filled with the Holy Spirit, we have the voice of God within us, speaking His loving counsel to help us. With all those voices inside, equally as distracting (if not even more)

---

[45] Matthew 7:7
[46] Exodus 3:4
[47] Exodus 19:19
[48] John 12:29, Acts 9:7
[49] 1 Kings 19:11-12

than if they were audible, we are in real need of training seasons to help us learn to better discern God's voice.

And that is why God leads us to wilderness times, so we can lean in to hear Him speak. Just as He would draw His people into a physical desert so they could give Him their undivided attention, far from the distracting temptations of comfort and societal expectations, so He allows internal wilderness seasons to shake us free from unhelpful influences and help us lean in to hear His voice on the inside. Just as Abraham, Moses, Elijah, David, and more Old Testament characters all spent considerable time learning to hear God's voice, so too did John the Baptist, Jesus, and Paul. And so too do we. This is where distractions and concerns about our surroundings become less important, and we become more aware of our need for His guidance if we are to survive.

Even though His still small internal voice can take a while to hear, and it is usually far less dramatic than it seemed in biblical accounts, the results are no less impactful. The voice of the Lord shakes the wilderness in today's opening verse. When God's voice is loud as thunder, that's easy to imagine. But even when it is internal, God's voice can split our dry season right open. Remember, He has not led us there (or allowed us to travel there) because He wants us to suffer, but because He wants us to learn. So, when we do learn to press in and discern His voice, we usually discover that what He is saying is the very thing we need to help us conquer this wilderness season.

It may be an utterance of His love, His presence with us, or His power to save. It may be a specific direction showing us the best next steps to take. It may be simply the assurance that He sees us and is able to speak to us. Whatever God says, it is always a blessing, even if it's a correction, because those come with immense grace and love. But the even bigger blessing is that God is speaking, because it shows we are in relationship still, and that is one of the most comforting reassurances I know. For as long as He is speaking and we can hear, we have hope that He can and will lead us through this place and out the other side.

So, I want to encourage you today: wilderness seasons are typically dry, lonely, and quiet. But God loves to meet us there, and He is always willing to speak. We just need to learn to lean in and listen for His still small voice. Keep listening, and He will help you hear.

N.B. For more on learning to hear God's voice, see Appendix 1.

Chapter 13 – Place of DESPERATION

*"She went on her way and wandered in the
Desert of Beersheba.
When the water in the skin was gone, she put the boy under
one of the bushes. Then she went off and sat down about a
bowshot away, for she thought, 'I cannot watch the boy die.'
And as she sat there, she began to sob."*
Genesis 21:14-16

THE BIBLICAL STORY of Hagar is not a comfortable read, as it speaks of her experiences as a slave. And yet there is beauty hidden in it too. Her master and mistress, Abram and Sarai, were godly people who had been given a promise from God that He would bless them with children. But they were barren – childless and well past the age of reproduction (Abram was eighty-six years old, Sarai ten years younger). Sarai's pain made her desperate, and she came up with a plan to achieve what God had promised: she would give her slave Hagar to her husband so he could have a child with her for Sarai to raise.

Whether or not Hagar consented to this is not mentioned. As a slave she had no rights, no voice or say in the matter. Abram slept with her, and they conceived a son. Once she knew she was carrying Abram's child, however, she obviously realised her value had increased, as she began to despise her barren mistress, Sarai, for being unable to give Abram what Hagar herself was carrying. Thus Sarai's pain was multiplied, so she treated Hagar so badly that the pregnant slave grew desperate enough to run away into the wilderness.

It is tempting to overlook Hagar as a minor character in the remarkable story of Abram and God's promise to make a great nation of his descendants. Some even see Hagar as a bit-part in the cautionary tale that is Sarai and Abram's attempt to help God with their own ideas. 'Trust God to bring His promises to pass,' we preach, 'and do not try to take control, lest you end up with an Ishmael' (reducing Abram's elder child to a mere mistake and blaming him for the pain his descendants would bring to God's chosen people). And poor Hagar does not even get a mention, just a used slave-girl who had to bear Abram's poor choice. But although she is invisible to us – a character with no rights and no obvious part in God's great plan – God saw her. His angel met her in the wilderness and sent her back, with a promise that He would make a mighty nation out of Ishmael's descendants.

So, Hagar was validated. Poor, overlooked, used-to-being-invisible, irrelevant Hagar declared, "I have now seen the One who sees me."[50] Suddenly she mattered – and so did her son.

Sometimes we find ourselves in a wilderness season because we are desperate: mistreated by others, rejected, or feeling invisible, like nobody sees our problems and nobody cares. Perhaps those who should have known better – God's own people – have been the source of our pain, making us feel like He is on their side and the only place available to us is this hostile land where we are all alone. But God always sees us. There is nowhere we can go where He cannot see us.[51] And when we are at our most desperate, that is when He finds us and sets us on the right path. If you have not found Him here yet, hold on – He's on His way.

Having met the God who saw her, Hagar returned to Abram and Sarai and gave birth to Ishmael there. The Bible makes no reference to Sarai bringing him up – he is always referred to as Hagar's son – which makes me suspect her confidence was boosted by God's promise,

---

[50] Genesis 16:13
[51] Psalm 139:7-12

allowing her to claim at least some rights as mother to Abram's child. And so, they all lived together until God appeared again to Abram and renewed His promise that he would become a mighty nation – but that the covenant would be established through his son with Sarai. And God changed their names to Abraham and Sarah, showing the promise was as good as done.

But Hagar? She got no mention. I wonder if she felt overlooked again, once more out of favour and irrelevant. And when ninety-year-old Sarah finally gave birth to their miracle son, Isaac, fourteen-year-old Ishmael was not happy. He taunted his little half-brother until Sarah persuaded Abraham to send Ishmael and Hagar away. Abraham loved his elder son, but God reassured him that He would care for him, and so Hagar found herself once again an outcast, ejected into the wilderness against her will. Fourteen years ago, God had told her to go back to her owners: had she done something wrong to make Him change His mind? Had He forgotten His promise now the favoured child was on the scene?

Now they were in an even more desperate place, with water and food running out. Teenage Ishmael was clearly in a bad way as Hagar laid him down under a bush and retreated so she did not have to watch him die. Personally speaking, I know of no greater despair as a mother than watching your own child suffer with no way of helping them. Desperation means you have lost hope of finding the thing you lack, whether that's water or the well-being of your child. Hagar had neither.

Did she remember the promise God had made all those years ago? She did not appear to have much faith as she resigned herself to losing Ishmael. But the God who sees all those in the wilderness had not forgotten them. As Hagar and her son wept separately, God's angel called to her from Heaven, asking what the matter was. He did not speak to Ishmael – the one with the promised destiny – He spoke to Hagar, the one He had met previously, and He reiterated His promise, meeting her again in her most desperate place to give fresh hope and remind her that she mattered too. Bit-part, overlooked Hagar mattered to God. Her example gives great hope to those feeling forgotten and unimportant! He sees us all. We may not feel like the main characters in God's story – the ones with the obvious call and destiny. But we matter too. He has blessings for us all; desires relationship with us all.

"Then God opened her eyes, and she saw a well of water."[52] Out of the whole story it is such a small part of a verse but makes all the difference, because it is the place where God met her desperation. He satisfied her physical thirst, and Ishmael's too – meaning that her son was also restored. But more than that, He satisfied her need to be seen, to matter, to have a life going forward. And how much more is that the case for those of us, thousands of years later, who now belong to an even better covenant. When we are in the wilderness, absolutely at the end of ourselves with desperation, feeling that if God does not come through for us there is no point going on – that is where He meets us. And He does not just call us by name and reiterate His promise as He did to Hagar; He does not just care for us in our place of felt need; He does not just give us a way out. He leads us to a well of living water.[53] The well He led Hagar to in the wilderness was enough to sustain them at least until they were strong enough to move on. But the well Jesus leads *us* to is one of everlasting, eternally thirst-quenching water – the water of God's own Holy Spirit.

So, I want to offer you this hope today, if you are in the place of desperation. Hang on – God will meet you there. Even if everyone else has forgotten you, He hasn't. He sees you. He calls you by name. He has a promise of meaning for your life. And He will lead you to His own well of living water for you to drink from for evermore. Hope will be restored – it is a promise.

---

[52] Genesis 21:19
[53] John 7:37-39

Chapter 14 – Place of ROMANCE

*"This is what the L*ORD *says: 'I remember the devotion of your youth, how as a bride you loved me and followed me through the wilderness, through a land not sown.'"*
Jeremiah 2:2

I REMEMBER THE day I first properly saw this verse. I had read it before, but this time it seemed to jump off the page and fly straight to my heart. It was the day I did a U-turn and really started to understand that the way God sees the wilderness – as somewhere beautiful – is entirely different to the way we tend to see it, as somewhere to be feared or avoided.

What mental picture do you imagine when you think of a wilderness? I picture a dry, bare, dusty place with little to no water, a few sparse scrubby plants, and an assortment of rocks scattered about. It is utterly hostile – not the kind of place we go for sightseeing, and certainly not for a romantic break! And yet that is the terminology God uses when talking about the wilderness: a place where His beloved followed Him in devotion, like a new bride on her honeymoon.

In this opening verse God was speaking to Israel about their forty years in the desert, when they followed His pillar of fiery cloud and learned to depend on Him for water, food, and clothing. His talk of their 'devotion' almost makes it sound like God is a misty-eyed romantic, especially considering that the time He was referring to was a season of almost constant complaining, foot-dragging, and longing for Egypt on the part of the Israelites. He had a far more charitable view of Israel at that time than I do, even though I can't kid myself that I would have been any better than them!

And yet when I looked closer, I found that despite Israel's long history of rebellion, there are moments of beautifully pure expressions of love from them to God. For example, when Moses came down Mount Sinai to Israel and asked them to make offerings for the purpose of building a tabernacle, the Israelites poured out such an offering in response that the leaders had to ask them to stop.[54] Imagine that: they were giving *too much!* Their offerings to God just kept coming, day after day, to the point where there was more than enough to fulfil the plans God had given Moses. For the first recorded time in history, Israel had given God more than He asked for! What a picture of overflowing adoration. No wonder God saw them as a devoted young bride.

Also, there is a hint in the words He used, describing how they loved *and* followed Him, as if their following is inextricably linked with their love. Interestingly, the word translated as 'follow' here is the Hebrew word *halak*, that means 'to walk'. It is the same word used for God walking in the garden of Eden,[55] Enoch walking with God,[56] righteous Noah walking with God,[57] and Abraham being called to walk blamelessly in God's presence.[58] It is clearly about walking in relationship. It reminds me of my generation in our youth: when we were dating a boyfriend/girlfriend, we were said to be 'going out with' them. I've heard other generations refer to it as 'stepping out with' or 'walking out with' their beloved. And here Israel was said to walk after/ walk with God, meaning just the same: they loved and followed Him, like a devoted young bride.

Then there's another passage that hints at their walk of love. In Numbers 9 we see how the Israelites followed God's cloud whenever it

---

[54] Exodus 36:3-7
[55] Genesis 3:8
[56] Genesis 5:24
[57] Genesis 6:9
[58] Genesis 17:1

moved and camped when it stayed still. Whether they had camped overnight, for a few days, or months, or even a year, they followed or camped with the cloud.[59] The phrase 'at the Lord's command they set out/encamped' is repeated over and over to hammer the point home: they followed God's every leading, every single time He moved. It was not just because they were lost – the journey across the desert was not unknown at the time, and at least some of them must have had an idea of where they were and how to get to civilisation. No, the people of Israel were following God's cloud because they *wanted* Him. However reluctant they were, however much they complained at times, however irritating it may have been to not know whether they were setting up camp for one night or a whole year, they still knew that God was worth following, and they chose the discomfort of walking after Him rather than making a break to find their own way. Difficult though the wilderness was, they knew life without God would be even worse – a bit like Jesus' disciples when He asked them if they wanted to leave, and they answered, "Where else would we go? Only you have the words of eternal life."[60] They – like Israel – were deeply uncomfortable, but they knew God was their only hope. And so, they kept following His lead – in Israel's case, for forty years. And God saw their walk after Him as demonstrating the devotion of a young bride.

So, perhaps surprisingly, Israel did show loving devotion to God in the hostile wilderness. And this place lends itself to that kind of romantic relationship building, because it is far from the public gaze. It's why God sometimes likes to hide here, as we saw in Chapter 7 – because there are aspects of His character He keeps private and only shares with those who love Him enough to seek Him out and follow Him through difficult spells. Developing trust in a relationship requires intimacy, and intimacy requires separation from others. And those forty years in the wilderness were a time when God had Israel to Himself, to develop their relationship of love, in private.

---

[59] Numbers 9:17-23
[60] John 6:68

FINDING JESUS IN THE WILDERNESS

And He calls us too, like the bridegroom in Song of Songs who called to his bride to follow him to a place of seclusion and intimacy: "Arise, my darling, my beautiful one, come with me."[61]

So yes, the wilderness *is* romantic and intimate. It may not feel comfortable to us, but we can be alone with God here. And when we remember we are alone *with* Him, it stops being a scary place and starts to become a place where we are free to learn devotion to Him and to discover how devoted He is to us. So, let's not waste this time by wishing for the end of this unpleasant season, when God is asking us to be secluded in the wilderness with Him for good reason. If we find ourselves crying out to God, 'When will this be over?', let's remember He doesn't want to rush, because this is a holy place where He takes His beloved to woo them. This wearying, barren desert is the place where He calls those who He wants to develop deeper relationship with. It's not a punishment; it's a picture of romantic devotion.

As God spoke to me once during a previous difficult season I wanted to end, '*Tarry a while, beloved. Time spent here with Me is never wasted, and we have many adventures to prepare for. Stay here with Me, that you may be made ready for what is to come. Learn to love deeper and be deeper loved in this place.*'

---

[61] Song of Songs 2:10

Chapter 15 – Place of QUESTIONING

"Then Jesus was led by the Spirit into the wilderness to be tempted by the devil. After fasting forty days and forty nights, he was hungry. The tempter came to him and said, 'If you are the Son of God, tell these stones to become bread.'"
Matthew 4:1-3

W E'VE LOOKED AT Jesus' forty days in the desert already, but there is another struggle common to most wilderness experiences hidden in the first specific temptation of Jesus. It's one of the devil's favourite, most insidious tactics: opening with doubt and questioning.

Let's look at his opening phrase: "If you are the Son of God…"

Even before launching into the actual temptations, the first words the enemy spoke were calculated to undermine Jesus' identity: "**If** you are the Son of God." At the baptism, God had affirmed aloud that Jesus was His Son, and now the enemy was directly challenging that. It was not the first time he used this tactic. In the Garden of Eden, Satan had introduced his temptation to Eve with a similarly nasty undermining question: "Did God **really** say…?"[62] And here he was questioning God's Word once more.

When we are in the wilderness, we might catch ourselves wondering, 'Do I **really** believe in God?', 'If He knows me, surely He can't really love me?', or 'Am I even a proper Christian?' We may feel

---

[62] Genesis 3:1

like we have lost our identity as a child of God. But we don't have to be afraid of those questions – often a reason for being here is so we can learn to answer them with more confidence. It is just not wise to attempt to reason with the enemy or engage with his questions as Eve tried to, or we could get lost wandering down a slippery and destructive path. We must take them to God and find our answers in His Word, the Bible. But we must never try to find the answer in how we feel – in this place our emotions will likely waver unreliably.

We may not *feel* anything except dry and weak, conscious of our most desperate need. As we saw in Chapter 9, Jesus was there too – "After fasting forty days and forty nights, he was hungry."[63] And at his point of feeling the weakest, here came the temptations. The devil does not wait for us to feel strong to tempt us; he does not play fair. He will wait until we feel dry and weak and then try to cause us to question if we even belong to God. But notice that Jesus did not even address the question of his identity or try to defend Himself – He just batted every temptation away with the truth found in God's Word – the only dependable answer to everything. We need to do as Jesus did and stand on what God has said, as recorded in the Bible, which is a truth far higher than our feelings! (Appendix 3 lists some scriptures to remind us of who we are in Christ.)

In my current wilderness, the original Garden of Eden question from the enemy has been the most persistent: "Did God really say…?" When we have walked with God for any length of time, we become familiar with seeking His guidance. As well as the general guidance found in His Word, we sometimes also seek specific, personal guidance for our lives, and when we feel we have heard from God, the words He gives are rich treasures to cling to. But in dry seasons like this the enemy comes with his sneaky questions, tempting us to wonder if God really said what we thought He said: did we hear Him, or were we making it up? The enemy knows that if he can get us to question whether we really heard God, the next logical step is to question

---

[63] Matthew 4:2

whether God is there at all. And that is what I have been experiencing in this season (more on that in Chapter 31).

When we believe God has given us personal guidance through His Holy Spirit, it is both important and wise to seek Him for confirmation – from His Word, and from trusted Christians around you (see Appendix 1). Once we have that confirmation, we set our faith and do not let go – holding onto it with an open hand, so God can still bring correction if needed, but also remembering that the promise will likely be challenged. The enemy does not want us to follow God's leading, so he often comes to undermine with questions that cause us to let go of God's promises. And when questions arise it is vital to have a heart like Jesus, standing on God's Word. And like Joshua and Caleb in their wilderness…

They were among the twelve spies who Moses sent to survey the Promised Land. Ten of them came back agreeing the land was all God said, but completely cowed by the circumstances – the giants already inhabiting it – and doubting God could do as He had promised. What He had said didn't matter, as it was impossible in their eyes. Only Joshua and Caleb pinned all their faith not on what they saw, but on the promise God had given them through Moses.[64] They saw the obstacles through God's eyes: impossible to man, but not to Him, and answered the question with faith: Yes, God can do what He promised. And consequently, they were the only ones who received that promise of their own land. Like Abraham, who considered the facts before him (that his body was 'as good as dead') but still firmly trusted that God was able to do what He had said.[65] If any of these men of God had wavered and let go of their promise, they would never have seen the fulfilment of it.

So, let's be encouraged today if we are facing questions. Let us bring the questions to God and be honest about them, and then let's find the answers – always – in His Word. If the circumstances around us cause us to question our identity in Christ or the words God has spoken to

---

[64] Numbers 14:6-9
[65] Romans 4:19-20

us, let's be sure to cry out to God for His strength, be honest about our struggles and seek confirmation if necessary, and follow Jesus' example to keep trusting and believing the truth in God's Word, for that alone is eternally, entirely dependable.

Chapter 16 – Place of REJOICING

"The desert and the parched land will be glad; the wilderness
will rejoice and blossom.
Like the crocus, it will burst into bloom; it will rejoice greatly
and shout for joy."
Isaiah 35:1-2

HEN WE ARE in a wilderness, the thought of rejoicing can
feel as unrelatable a concept as the thought of a dry and
dusty desert suddenly bursting into bloom across the land:
it is ridiculous, almost offensive. And yet this is what God promises.
The above passage from Isaiah is generally taken as referring to the end
times when Jesus restores His Kingdom in all its fullness, eradicating
dry and barren places forever. It can also be taken as referring to
unbelievers who receive His life when they are born again. But many
times, God can and does also use His 'big picture' prophecies to speak
into our individual situations. It makes sense: His principles remain
the same in every area of life, big or small. And so, His promise of
restoring life and rejoicing in the desert applies to each one of us in our
wilderness seasons too.

Recently my family received some news. We have been praying for
a needed miracle as we are in an impossible situation but believe God
has promised breakthrough. The other day we received a message that
seemed to absolutely shut down any chance of the miracle we were
believing for, denying all our hopes and God's promise. It came on a

day when I was exhausted on many levels from petty things going wrong at home, relationally and practically, and the message wiped me out. I had no reserves left to deal with it, so with a very heavy heart I went to my room, shut the door, and just wept, crying out for help: "Jesus, I need You." Immediately I heard His voice… laughing. I was stunned – it seemed to cut right across my sad and heavy heart. I could have been offended that He was not sympathetic enough to join me in my pity-party, but as I heard the joy in His voice, I realised He was not laughing *at* me, but *over* me. His laughter was not unkind or mocking, it was a blessing and an invitation that lifted me out of my pit. And the more I leaned into His laughter, the less weak and exhausted I felt.

Please do not read this the wrong way. If we as Christians habitually approached our struggling friends and just laughed, or tried to force them to cheer up, that would be deeply insensitive and inappropriate. Those experiencing wilderness seasons rarely feel joyful, and that is not something to be chastised or corrected, but rather something to bring to God who understands and wants to extend mercy, walking with us even in the valleys. As the Bible says, trying to force superficial cheer onto someone who is struggling is as insulting as taking a coat of an already cold person.[66] But that is not what was happening to me.

I believe God knew in this rare situation that unlike the many times when He just listened and ministered love and compassion to me, this time I needed something else. And of course He was right. As He laughed, I understood that He was not exhausted or worried about my situation, and neither was He allowing me to get bogged down in self-pity. Although He was – and is always – compassionate towards me in my weakness, He knew at that moment I needed His strength – the joy of the Lord is always our strength.[67] And so, He laughed, rejoicing because He can see the truth of our coming answer to prayer. He was laughing with joy at the promise we are still to receive. And, as I sat and listened to His laugh echoing around my spirit, I felt strength and

---

[66] Proverbs 25:20
[67] Nehemiah 8:10

faith overtaking my previous sense of weak exhaustion. It still gives me strength now as we wait for the promise to arrive.

I shared this with a dear friend who was initially shocked at my experience of Jesus laughing. She wondered why He would not just hold me with compassion and sympathy as He has done so many times before. But then I shared something I wrote about in *Friend of God*. A large part of my story is the way God transformed me from lack to fruitfulness, literally making this childless woman a happy mother of children.[68] Through six years of a deeply difficult barren wilderness season, every time I started to feel I might be experiencing early pregnancy symptoms that turned out to be false, I struggled afresh. God had promised us children, so I did my best to cling to hope, but sometimes it felt so far away. And then one day, feeling utterly exhausted and concluding I must have glandular fever, I lay down and complained to God about how hard it was. But instead of meeting me with compassion for my suffering as He had so many times before, He gave a gentle laugh and said, *'You were always going to have pregnancy symptoms that turned out to be real one day!'* His laugh was not unsympathetic but came from a higher place, reassuring me of His joy that we would be sharing in very soon. And indeed we did – within the week I had taken a test and discovered I was pregnant with our first miracle baby! And because we had been trying and hoping for so long, our house was quickly filled with congratulatory bouquets of flowers from friends who had been praying with us, now rejoicing at our transformation from barrenness to fruitfulness. The flowers that filled our house (we had to borrow vases to put them in, there were so many) were a beautiful picture of this chapter's opening verse of blooms erupting in the wilderness. We came to rejoice in our changed circumstances, but Jesus had access to that joy all along.

See, joy is not the same as happiness. Happiness is a fickle feeling that usually depends on our circumstances – the people we are with, the things happening around us, our needs being met. But joy is the very nature of God: deep and unchangeable because HE is

---

[68] Psalm 113:9

unchangeable. We rejoice not because of our shifting circumstances but because of who He is: loving, patient, kind, forgiving, good, faithful, gentle… and because He is for us! Circumstances may change, but thanks to Jesus' sacrifice, God's goodwill towards us never does. So even when times are hard, we can rejoice. Even if we do not *feel* particularly happy, we can choose to remember His goodness and faithfulness. It is a peculiar paradox that we can rejoice even while still feeling sad or dry. Because rejoicing is reminding ourselves of the truth about God that will eventually turn this barren land into a place that blooms. It might not *feel* like happiness, but it still counts as rejoicing when we remember His goodness.

Rejoicing in the wilderness is refreshing. It can be awkward and uncomfortable at first, like exercising a muscle we have forgotten we had, but if we ask God for help, He loves to answer. With the Holy Spirit within us, we always have access to the fruit of joy. Sometimes it can get buried under self-pity or hopelessness, and then we need to make a determined effort to take our eyes off our depressing circumstances and turn them to Jesus – everything He is and everything He has done for us! It is not about forcing it or 'fake it 'til you make it' – that would be counter-productive. God wants our authentic hearts, not a show of misguided performance. But if we turn to Him and ask Him to help us rejoice even in difficult times, He will answer. Authentically. And the more we do this, the more quickly we will regain His joy and strength, and faith will be restored, like unlikely flowers blooming in a desert.

And again, if you're not here yet, don't worry or feel condemned. It is coming – just cry out for help, and you will receive your answer in time.

Chapter 17 – Place of FAILURE

*"Now Moses was tending the flock of Jethro his father-in-law,
the priest of Midian, and he led the flock to the far side of the
wilderness and came to Horeb, the mountain of God. There
the angel of the LORD appeared to him in flames of fire from
within a bush."*

Exodus 3:1-2

EIGHTY-YEAR-OLD Moses had lived in the wilderness for half his life. His golden days of privilege in Egypt were a distant memory. He had fled to exile in Midian long ago, and for the past four decades he had lived there, finding a wife, having children, and generally settling for a life of obscurity tending his father-in-law's sheep.

The Bible says little about the first part of his life when he lived in Egypt as a child. We know he was hidden from sight for a while due to the Egyptian policy of killing newborn Hebrew boys,[69] and then at three months old when he could no longer be hidden, his mother placed him in a basket at the edge of the river where Pharaoh's daughter found him.[70] Moses' sister, who was watching, offered to find a nurse who could feed the baby for the princess, and Moses was reunited with his family for a while but no longer hidden. Now the princess was paying them to keep him alive until he was weaned, when

---

[69] Exodus 1:22
[70] Exodus 2:5-6

he would be returned to her to be brought up as her son.[71] Thus from his earliest years, he was clearly marked for something special. The Bible does not tell us anything about his time in the palace, except that he was educated in all the wisdom of the Egyptians and was powerful in speech and action.[72] What we do know is that somehow and at some point, he was made aware of his Hebrew identity, of God, *and* of a sense of responsibility to deliver his people. See Acts 7:23-25:

"When Moses was forty years old, he decided to visit his own people, the Israelites. He saw one of them being mistreated by an Egyptian, so he went to his defence and avenged him by killing the Egyptian. Moses thought that his own people would realise that God was using him to rescue them, but they did not."

Somehow Moses knew he had been saved for a reason – that his life of privilege and wealth, education and power was for a purpose that involved God working through him to save his people. And yet when he acted towards that purpose, it all went horribly wrong. His people, the Israelites, rejected him,[73] and Pharaoh, whose family Moses had been brought up in, did the same and worse, declaring a death sentence against him.[74] In that moment Moses went from feeling a call on his life to use his privileged position to save Israel, to being twice-outcast, with no power or influence left, only death if he remained. So, he fled and ended up tending sheep in the wilderness for forty years! I wonder if he thought he had ruined his chance to fulfil God's call, and if – far from God's people and surrounded by idol-worshippers – he felt God had given up on him. Human experience tells me that is most likely, and that for forty years he probably lived without hope of anything beyond failure and exile...

How many of us have had times in our lives when we had a sense of the good plans God had for us there? Exciting plans that might take us out of our comfort zone but would put our gifts and our experience to beneficial use? We long to discover what we were created for, and

---

[71] Exodus 2:8-10
[72] Acts 7:22
[73] Exodus 2:14
[74] Exodus 2:15

when we think we have found it, we cannot wait to get started. But then when something unexpected happens and it looks like we have missed our chance to do remarkable things for God, we blame ourselves for whatever happened, rightly or wrongly, and write ourselves off, forever. That sense of failure is one that heads straight into the wilderness – I've experienced that. Have you?

Moses dwelt in obscurity for forty years, crushed and with no aspirations – all sense of privilege and/or calling long gone. Until one day, when leading his father-in-law's flock to the back of beyond, he saw something impossible: a bush on fire that was not being burned up. He went for a closer look, and God spoke to him there, calling him to return to Egypt and deliver His people.[75] Note that long ago Moses had seen Israel as his own people – now they were *God's* people. From that and the conversation that followed, we can clearly see that any sense of pride or entitlement Moses may have once had was all gone. Now he was full of protestation, 'buts', and 'I can'ts'. Failure and impossibility were now fully part of his identity. But the God who restores all would not take no for an answer. Right from the beginning he had set Moses aside for a purpose. That purpose had taken longer than Moses expected, but God never forgot (He is always in far less of a hurry than we are), and now He had come to call Moses back to his original, God-given purpose.

How gracious God is! How kind to restore us when we feel we have failed and messed up our lives so they cannot be fixed. God can *always* redeem our messes. Even when we have lived in the wilderness for so long it has become our entire identity like Moses, God will do whatever it takes to get our attention and restore us back to Himself. And so, in that single desert encounter, God interrupted Moses' established view of himself as a failure and called him back to purpose. Only this time Moses knew he could not do this in his own strength: he had no power or privilege of his own to rely on. He would have to rely fully on God – which is exactly how it needed to be.

---

[75] Exodus 3:10

I dare say Moses needed to fail. He needed to be confronted with his own inability to carry out what God had called him to, otherwise the signs and wonders that God would perform in Egypt could be contaminated by a sense of pride, possibly ruining the whole plan. But here and now, pride had been so thoroughly stripped from Moses that he genuinely believed God needed to ask someone better qualified. And God knew He could work through someone who would give Him ALL the glory for what would follow.

So, if you are in the wilderness right now because of a failure – because you feel you messed up what you thought God was leading you to – I want to encourage you today, this is not the end. The God who restored Moses and worked through him so powerfully is the same God who will restore you too. You may have written yourself off, but He has not. He knows where to find you and how to get your attention, and He still has good plans and purposes for you.[76] Don't give up – He's on His way.

---

[76] Jeremiah 29:11

Chapter 18 – Place of BEING CARRIED

*"In the wilderness… you saw how the L*ORD *your God*
carried you,
as a father carries his son, all the way you went until you
reached this place."
Deuteronomy 1:31

I LOVE THE imagery of this verse: we've surely all seen, if not experienced for ourselves, how a father tenderly carries his child when they cannot walk any further, whether from tiredness or injury. And the truth is, when we have wilderness seasons, we often feel overwhelmed with weakness, pain or discouragement, and simply cannot carry on. In those times of defeat God does not chide, discipline or correct. Instead, He does not hesitate to scoop us up and carry us, holding us close to His chest where we can feel His heartbeat and know we are safe.

It reminds me of the well-known piece of writing called 'Footprints' (author unknown)[77] that describes someone's walk with God. They dreamed or envisioned scenes from their life appearing in the sky and saw two sets of footprints in the sand beneath, representing their footsteps walking alongside those of Jesus. But when they came to the most painful and difficult parts of their life, they noticed there was only one set of footprints. Troubled, they asked God why He left them

---

[77] Despite my best efforts, I have not been able to establish the authorship of the poem with any certainty as it is at the centre of ongoing legal dispute. Should this change, I will be happy to give full credit where it is due.

during their seasons of greatest need, and He replied, 'My precious child, I never left you. Those times when you only saw one set of footprints reveal the times when I carried you.'

It is just the most beautiful picture of the Father heart of God, who never condemns us for our weakness but willingly carries us until we can stand again.

When Moses originally declared our opening verse, it was at the end of Israel's journey across the wilderness: they had been travelling for forty years, and now Moses was recounting everything that had happened so that none would forget. In Chapter 14 we saw how God viewed those years with fondness, remembering Israel's bride-like devotion to Him. Now we have Moses recounting the same time through the lens of a different relationship, viewing Israel as a helpless child. It makes me smile, as I remember many family walks when my own children were small. With three young boys I found it essential to go for regular walks so they could burn off some energy rather than taking it out on each other or innocent household items. Sometimes they would resist and complain as we started walking, but if we kept going, they would usually come round and enjoy themselves. Most times the aim was two-fold: to have fun exploring somewhere new as a family, and to walk until they were tired, doing our best to time it so they were tired enough to have used up their surplus energy, but not so much that they became emotionally overwhelmed and argumentative.

So, if taking my children for walks was for their physical and mental wellbeing, and to get some quality time together, it seems to me that God had a similar view of Israel. Of course, He had a practical goal to deliver them to the Promised Land and thus save them from slavery. But if we think about it with a wider lens, we can see it is also a picture of His Father heart for *us*: how He wants to deliver us from lives of slavery to sin, into His Kingdom. And He does that by taking us for a walk, teaching us lessons along the way. We, like children, think the lessons are small and separate, like learning the rules (whether that be the Ten Commandments or the Countryside Code), and being able to identify different flora and fauna, and recognising the signs of impending harsh weather. But the overall lesson is this: we have a good Father who delights to be with us. Even when we start off in a bad mood, He perseveres until we relax and can see the joy of being with Him. And if we stumble or grow too weary to continue, He does not reprimand us or leave us alone – He carries us. Just like my husband and I did with our boys. Just like God did with the nation of Israel as He led them through the wilderness, providing food and water, leading them every step of the way, teaching them all they needed to know, especially about relationship with Him.

Quite simply, He wants all of us to walk with Him. That is why He created us. And if the journey grows too hard as it sometimes does, our loving Father will carry us close to Him until we can walk again.

Chapter 19 – Place of DELAY

*"These are the words that Moses spoke to all the people of Israel
while they were in the wilderness east of the Jordan River…
Normally it takes only eleven days to travel from Mount
Sinai to Kadesh-barnea, going by way of Mount Seir. But
forty years after the Israelites left Egypt… Moses addressed the
people of Israel, telling them everything the L*ORD* had
commanded him to say."*
Deuteronomy 1:1-3 (NLT)

THERE IS SOME jaw-dropping information in these opening verses of Deuteronomy. Israel's journey across the desert could/should have taken them only eleven days, but it took them forty years! We know the reason: of the twelve spies sent to check out the Promised Land, only two of them came back with faith and trust in God to do what He had said. The other ten came back with fear, viewing the worldly circumstances as stronger than God. And, when all Israel listened to the faithless ones and started up their complaining and rebellion again, God vowed that none of the people who had chosen fear over faith would ever enter the Promised Land.[78] Their punishment was to wander the wilderness for the following forty years, waiting for a new generation to arise and take their place. That's a serious delay!

---

[78] Deuteronomy 1:35

In my current season, I think I have camped longer at this place of delay than anywhere else. It is one of the most frustrating and discouraging places to be, knowing there is nothing we can do to move on except wait for God's timing and trust Him. I am thankful that even when our own mistakes bring us to the place of delay, those of us in Christ are no longer being punished like the Israelites were. Jesus has been punished for all our sin, so we know that whatever brought us here, we are not stuck here until we die.

And yet, Proverbs 13:12 says, "Hope postponed grieves the heart." (VOICE)

When we are praying and waiting and praying and waiting for Jesus to deliver us from the wilderness, and the delay just drags on and on, our hearts grieve, and it becomes harder than ever to hold onto hope.

There was a day when I was pouring out my heart to God in prayer but without much faith that I would hear a response as I was in that place of grieving, tempted to feel that the delay was either because of something I had done wrong or something right I had failed to do (you know how it goes). And to my relief, God answered. I felt prompted to share the response here, because I believe it is for some of you too:

*'Beloved, that voice inside that says you must be doing something wrong or not doing enough – that is not My voice. You could never do enough to deserve or be worthy of Me: that is why **I** have done it all. You do not have to do anything except believe and receive. You don't have to search around for mistakes and cracks to fill, as if prayer were a monument that has to be perfect before I will answer. Answered prayer does not come from you getting the formula right; it is simply about you talking to Me in relationship and trusting that I care enough to respond. The cry of your heart to Me is all the prayer I need. You are righteous in Christ, so I always answer.*[79]

I was comforted, but still struggling, so I asked, 'If our prayers are so powerful, why then do we have to persist in prayer when the answer is delayed?'

---

[79] James 5:16

He replied, *'Because we have an enemy who tries to get in the way.[80] But also because many times the issue is about what I am forming in you during the delay: strength, patience, trust. If you were not able to persevere in faith it would mean you had quit, which is rarely positive. But when you persevere it is a sign that you have not let go of faith. Repeated prayer exercises your faith muscle and builds trust. Sometimes these repetitive exercises are painful (that's how muscle develops) and you must dig deep to push through. Whether you persevere out of deep desire and connection or just because you know you must, the result is the same: you persevere. Sometimes when you become exhausted you need to rest between sets of repetitions – that applies to physical exercise **and** prayer – but I am a good trainer. I know when to let you rest and when to motivate you to get going again. Perseverance in prayer builds strong faith. Do not undervalue this time, beloved.'*

So, it's not that God wants us to suffer or for our hearts to grieve when the answers to our prayers are delayed. But He is committed to helping us grow stronger, and one of the best ways to grow strong in faith is through repeatedly crying out to Him in prayer and learning to trust Him even in the delay. Like Romans 5:3-5 tells us, "Suffering produces perseverance; perseverance, character, and character, hope."

Jesus told a parable about perseverance to His disciples "to show them that they should always pray and not give up".[81] We know it as The Parable of the Persistent Widow – the woman who pestered the unrighteous judge so frequently that he finally gave in and did what she asked.[82] And, as Jesus pointed out, God IS righteous, so we are even more certain of Him answering. But the ultimate point of the parable, that is often overlooked, is found at the end where Jesus concludes with, "However, when the Son of Man comes, will He find faith on the earth?"[83] The whole point of persevering in prayer is to produce faith.

---

[80] Daniel 10:12-13
[81] Luke 18:1
[82] Luke 18:2-8
[83] Luke 18:8

When we are in the middle of a season of delay, it can feel like our faith is being leached from us: the longer we wait for the hope that we desire, the harder it is to believe we will see the answer. But it is that difficulty, and our hanging on through it all, that exercises our faith and trust in God and ultimately makes us stronger.

And remember, the second half of Proverbs 13:12 brings a beautiful conclusion to the postponed hope, reminding us that all difficult seasons eventually end, and what seems like a vague dream will become a solid reality: "Hope postponed grieves the heart; but when a dream comes true, life is full and sweet."[84]

However delayed it may be in the wilderness, we WILL receive our answer in the end, so don't quit!

---

[84] Proverbs 13:12 (VOICE)

Chapter 20 – Place of
MIRACULOUS PROVISION

"Our ancestors ate the manna in the wilderness;
as it is written:
'He gave them bread from heaven to eat.'"
John 6:31

THERE ARE MANY very real problems and difficulties to be found in the wilderness, but the blessing contained in today's chapter is a constant theme running through Israel's forty-year journey: when all natural possibilities have been exhausted and there are no options left, we find God there, generously and miraculously providing everything needed.

Many years ago, I taught in a Christian preschool. Trying to explain divine concepts to three-year-olds can be a challenge, but it can reveal great treasures too. And one day, when explaining miracles to my preschoolers, I found myself giving them a simple definition that has stayed with me ever since: 'A miracle is when God does something impossible.'

People use the word 'miracle' today to mean all sorts of amazing or fortunate occurrences. I tend to call my sons miracles because my husband and I had previously been told by medical professionals that the chances of us conceiving were next-to-nothing. But still, there was an infinitesimally tiny chance, and we were doing what we needed to do, so the birth of our babies was not on the same level of impossibility as Jesus being born to a virgin.

But whatever our definition of miracle, it cannot be denied that many aspects of Israel's journey through the wilderness were entirely miraculous. God provided water when there was none;[85] He made their shoes and clothes last forty years of hard travel through a desert without wearing out;[86] and when there was no food to eat, He not only provided meat through a flock of quail that blew in,[87] but also – and perhaps most miraculously of all – provided manna for bread.[88] The flakes of manna that appeared on the ground might have seemed like a natural phenomenon were it not for a specific detail: God told Israel to gather twice as much as they needed on the sixth day, so that they would not need to work to collect it on the seventh day of ordained Sabbath rest. On any other day if the Israelites collected too much, the manna would become infested with maggots overnight.[89] But on the seventh day – no maggots. It kept perfectly. However, if they went out to gather manna on the Sabbath day, there would be none. It only appeared six days out of seven.[90] We can try to logically explain away any of the other provisions, but logic does not cut it with the manna. It was not a natural phenomenon – it was undeniably supernatural. Miraculous, in fact.

Plus, of course, the whole wilderness experience started and ended with two miraculous partings of water: first, the Red Sea,[91] and last, the flooded River Jordan.[92] And not to forget the manifest presence of God that led them every step of the way, in the form of a pillar of cloud by day and fire by night.[93] And even that didn't conclude the long list of miracles – there were the Ten Commandments, divinely inscribed

---

[85] Exodus 17:3-6
[86] Deuteronomy 29:5
[87] Numbers 11:31
[88] Exodus 16:2-5
[89] Exodus 16:20
[90] Exodus 16:25-27
[91] Exodus 14:21-27
[92] Joshua 3:14-17
[93] Exodus 13:21-22

onto stone tablets (twice![94]), the bronze snake on a pole that healed everyone who looked at it,[95] the defeat of the Amalekites when they attacked Israel, losing the battle only because Moses' hands were raised to God[96]… the miracles went on and on.

The point is clear: we may be in a dry, barren, and lonely place with no possible natural comfort or provision, but that just means it is the perfect backdrop for an 'impossible' miracle. It is a place where *any* provision must be miraculous – it can only come from God. And God loves to meet us there.

But it strikes me that with all the miracles there was also a step of faith required. Israel had to set foot between the waters – they could have chosen to give in to fear and not moved (at least through the Jordan… with the Egyptian army hot on their heels they had little choice with the Red Sea crossing). With the manna, they had to gather it every day; when the Amalekites attacked they still had to fight; when the pillar of cloud and fire moved, they still had to make the choice to follow it; Moses had to follow God's instructions to obtain the water; they had to turn their focus away from self-pity and lift their eyes to look at the bronze snake for healing.

When we are in a wilderness season, we can be confident that God is there and that He is willing to miraculously provide for whatever we need. We just need to remember that accessing His miracles can require something of us too. It may be a step of faith – to follow the leading of His Holy Spirit, even when He takes us in a different direction to the one we expect. It may be as simple as turning our gaze away from self-pity to focus on Him and what He can do. Perhaps it requires a choice to stop obsessing so much on the big deliverance miracle that will get us out of here in order to notice and value all the 'smaller' (actually more important) miracles of God daily walking with us through this difficult season. Or it may require us to embrace the daily discipline of getting up in the morning to gather our daily bread from Heaven.

---

[94] Exodus 32:15-16 & Ex 34:1
[95] Numbers 21:8-9
[96] Exodus 17:8-13

And here is where we discover the most beautiful miraculous provision of all. For we know Israel's forty-year journey is in some ways a picture for us representing our time here on earth: longing for the Promised Land of eternity in God's Kingdom, but still earthbound, struggling through this life in a hostile realm. And even here, God provides our daily bread… that is, Jesus.

"'It is not Moses who has given you the bread from heaven, but it is my Father who gives you the true bread from heaven. For the bread of God is the bread that comes down from heaven and gives life to the world.'… Then Jesus declared, '**I am the bread of life**. Whoever comes to me will never go hungry, and whoever believes in me will never be thirsty.'" (John 6:32-35 – emphasis mine)

We know Jesus spent forty days and nights in the wilderness, echoing Israel's forty years. Clearly, He knows what it is like to hunger and thirst for physical food, and He knows how desperately we need Him to be our spiritual food and drink, without which we would be spiritually dead. The miracle of our desert experience is this: Jesus is the answer to our every need. He teaches us to pray for daily bread, and then, when we get up each morning to gather it, He meets us in that place so we can receive all the nourishment we need from Him.

So, Jesus is our manna in the wilderness. He will give us all we need, one day at a time, to keep us going until we reach our Promised Land, whether that be the end to this temporary dry season or the 'bigger picture' end of our life on this earth. Whatever the difficulty, He is the miracle we need, and He will provide the miracles we need. Always.

Chapter 21 – Place of TESTING

*"Remember how the Lord your God led you all the way in the
wilderness these forty years, to humble and test you in order to
know what was in your heart,
whether or not you would keep his commands."*
Deuteronomy 8:2

WE HAVE LOOKED at a chapter on temptation, and now we
come to testing, which may feel similar but is not the same
thing. Put very simply, it can help to categorise temptation
as something the enemy does to us, wanting us to fail and fall away
from God, while testing is something that God does to us, to help us
succeed and grow closer to Him. The Hebrew word for test, *nasah,* can
also be translated as 'prove': our response to the test proves what is in
our hearts and allows God to prove that when we trust Him, He will
meet us there.

Both tempting and testing are uncomfortable; both carry an
element of risk depending on our response. But testing, unlike
temptation, is designed not for failure but to reveal the gold inside, as
part of the process. As God said in Zechariah 13:9, "I will refine them
like silver and test them like gold. They will call on my name and I will
answer them; I will say, 'They are my people,' and they will say,
'The Lord is our God.'"

So, we see testing is an important part of our lives when we walk with God. He does it so we can more fully know we belong to Him.[97] Abraham was tested when God asked him to sacrifice his beloved son Isaac. God never intended for Isaac to die (and made sure he didn't), but He tested Abraham to *prove* that Abraham loved God above anything else. The gold of Abraham's faith was fully proven, and the stage was set for God to later give HIS beloved Son in sacrifice, proving that He loves us more than anything else.

When it comes to natural procedures for testing gold, I learned there are five basic tests that are commonly used[98] – each of which I believe can give helpful parallels in relation to God testing for the gold of faith in our hearts:

1. *Measuring and weighing gold will reveal it as more dense and weightier than most other metals.*
   How weighty is our faith? When we are tested in the wilderness, does our faith anchor us and prove to be solid and enduring, or is it light and wavering, easily overcome?

2. *Gold is not magnetic. If a strong magnet can pick it up, it is not pure gold but has been mixed with other metals.*
   Are we set apart and holy for God? Tests can reveal if He alone has our heart or if we have allowed our faith to be contaminated by the cares of the world and/or the opinions of others.

3. *Gold produces a long, high-pitched ringing sound when struck. More base metals sound dull and shorter.*
   When we are struck with a test, what sound do we make? A dull moan of bitter complaint, or does our faith ring out in praise of our Lord?

---

[97] Genesis 22:1-2

[98] Thanks to https://www.bullionbypost.co.uk/index/gold/how-to-tell-if-gold-is-real/ Feb 22, 2021

4. *Gold leaves a gold mark on a ceramic plate when dragged across it. Fake gold leaves a black mark.*

   The tests we go through often leave a mark on those we come into contact with – does what they see in us glorify God, or is it polluted with sin?

5. *Gold resists oxidation and corrosion. If it reacts to (nitric) acid, it is not gold. There are different strengths of acid for different carats of gold – the purest that does not react at all being 24 carat.*

   How pure is our faith? There are diverse levels of test that reveal the purity of our faith – the more we endure, and allow ourselves to be refined, the purer we will become.

I know these tests are not easy – nothing in the wilderness is. They require humility and openness to God convicting us where we fall short (not an easy attitude to have, especially here where there is no comfortable counsellor's couch to recline upon, only discomfort and hardship). But remember, God is not seeking to condemn us for failing – only to prove our faith and make us more like Jesus. These tests may not be comfortable to go through, but if we will open our hearts before God and submit to His testing, He has promised He will reveal His gold. He is committed to doing a deep work in us and will not leave us unfinished.[99]

So, I hope and pray that if you have found yourself at the place of testing, you will take courage from knowing God is right there with you in it, forming Jesus within you, for His glory. Because when God tests for gold, He does not give up until He has it.

"With this hope you can be happy even if you need to have sorrow and all kinds of tests for a while. These tests have come to prove your faith and to show that it is good. Gold, which can be destroyed, is

---

[99] Philippians 1:6

tested by fire. Your faith is worth much more than gold and it must be tested also."[100]

So we pray,
"God, examine me and know my heart;
test me and know my anxious thoughts.
See if there is any bad thing in me.
Lead me on the road to everlasting life. "[101]

And, as the road that led us to this time of testing in the wilderness was designed to lead us back to God, we can take heart: He will not let us fail!

[100] 1 Peter 1:6-7 NLV
[101] Psalm 139:23-24 NCV

Chapter 22 – Place of CONNECTION

*"The Lᴏʀᴅ said to Aaron, 'Go into the wilderness to meet
Moses.' So he met Moses at the mountain of God and
kissed him. Then Moses told Aaron everything the Lᴏʀᴅ had
sent him to say, and also about all the signs he had
commanded him to perform."*
Exodus 4:27-28

Tᴏᴅᴀʏ's ᴄʜᴀᴘᴛᴇʀ ᴄᴏᴠᴇʀs one of my favourite wilderness blessings – especially considering that one of the most common associations with this place is that of loneliness (see Chapter 11). Yes, this is a lonely place, and that means spending any amount of time here makes fellowship even more precious when we find it.

In today's opening verses, Moses had been away for a long time. The last time Aaron had seen him was at least forty years ago. And now, with no idea where his brother had been for the last four decades, God told Aaron to go into the wilderness to find him – and he did! A lot is said about Moses encountering God face to face, but I find it impressive that Aaron not only heard God but obeyed Him. I would love to know how he knew where to look. Did God tell him exactly where to go from the outset, or did He lead him as he went? Either way, Moses was not the only one having a wilderness experience: Aaron was trusting God with his own desert journey too.

And of course, in the meantime Moses was talking to God in the form of a fiery bush. God was calling Moses to go and deliver his people, just as he had dreamed of doing long ago.[102] But as we saw in Chapter 17, forty years of wilderness exile had left him with zero confidence: "Who am I to do this?"[103] And when God responded to convince him that He would go with him, Moses kept arguing back until he finally asked God to send someone else. God was not impressed with the continuous excuses – but even in His anger He revealed He had already made provision to overcome Moses' qualms, saying, "[Aaron] is already on his way to meet you, and he will be glad to see you."[104] Suddenly Moses' objections dried up, and he went to tell his father-in-law he was leaving.

Sometimes even the knowledge that God goes with us is not enough. Sometimes we need human help too – and God knows that. He knows how to connect us with others who can help us to fulfil what we have been asked to do. And it is not always the people around us. Sometimes God sends us someone from a long way away who has been on a wilderness journey of their own. Because there's something about travelling through dry deserts that marks us, rubbing off any sense of entitlement or superiority. It levels us all to a state of humble gratitude to God for bringing us through. We know that our life is not in our hands, and we have nothing to prove – and so when two people connect who have been through the same process of having their pride and positioning stripped away, then God is able to work through them together mightily.

So, these two wilderness wanderers met each other at the mountain and shared everything God had been revealing. Then they returned to Israel and told the elders all God had said. And the elders believed.[105] From that point on, Moses and Aaron worked as a team – and regardless of which of them spoke or performed a miracle at any point,

---

[102] Acts 7:25
[103] Exodus 3:11
[104] Exodus 4:14
[105] Exodus 4:31

either way Israel (and Egypt) were left in no doubt: this was a work of God, and only He received the glory for it all.

I find it fascinating that despite Moses' insistence that he was unable to speak, and claims to need somebody to speak for him, once he received Aaron's partnership and they stood before Pharaoh together, Aaron did not do all the speaking. When we read through the chapters of Exodus, we see that sometimes Aaron spoke, sometimes Moses did. Sometimes Aaron lifted his staff to perform miracles; sometimes Moses did. Clearly God did not send Aaron to replace Moses, but to co-labour with him. They became like one in their ministry. Even though Moses was the one with the call of God, who spoke with Him face to face, Aaron was the essential support who gave him strength to do all that God had asked him to.

Sometimes the wilderness leaves us broken and scarred, struggling to believe we can do what He asks. Even then God knows how to restore us, and sometimes that is through sending us co-labourers who can help us regain strength in God. And when He connects us with others who have been on similar journeys, I believe the connection goes deeper than normal friendships. Self-importance is mostly stripped away by the wilderness, and those who emerge tend to be more inclined to humility and serving God (and each other) rather than pursuing their own priorities.

It may be that our dry season has stripped us of all confidence. That is not necessarily a terrible thing: we need to learn to have confidence in God and not ourselves, knowing we can do nothing good in ourselves but with Him working through us, all things are possible! And yet, there may be a season when God restores us by sending someone to walk with us for a while. He has sent me some people like this throughout my life. And I've found there are a few qualities that can help us to identify them as sent by God:

- Humility. They are not here to promote themselves but to serve God.

- Servant-heartedness. They don't talk about themselves and their calling all the time but are willing to help us grow in our calling too, as we are for them. This calling may even be the same for a while.

- Prayerfulness. They know our mutual success depends not on them, but on both of our relationships with God.

- Like-mindedness. In our spirit we recognise them as one marked by the wilderness, with a similar journey and calling as our own.

These co-labourers are such a gift and encouragement when we meet them. But do be aware that working together for the rest of our lives, as Moses and Aaron did, is not a guarantee. Sometimes the seasons of working together are shorter than others. But even when the season ends and we are called in different directions, we part in love and those God-given connections remain as a blessing that bears eternal fruit.

So, if God connects you with a wilderness traveller for a season, I pray for grace and mutual encouragement that will set His people free, as surely as Moses and Aaron together led Israel to liberty. Amen.

Chapter 23 – Place of HUMBLING

*"Remember how the LORD your God led you all the way in the
wilderness these forty years, to humble and test you in order to
know what was in your heart,
whether or not you would keep his commands."*
Deuteronomy 8:2

ALTHOUGH WE HAVE previously looked at the wilderness as a
place of testing, there is a second purpose for desert seasons
that is spelt out in this verse, and it is for humbling. But it is
important to recognise from the outset that humbling is not the same
as humiliation. To be humiliated is to be exposed so everyone can see
our shame. But when God humbles us, it is typically a private act: He
covers us from the gaze of others while He brings correction.
Thankfully, it is the reason He tends to use the wilderness to humble
us: it is secluded and hidden from public view and humiliation.

Deuteronomy 8:3 – the verse after our opening verse – describes
how this humbling happened to Israel: "He humbled you, causing you
to hunger and then feeding you with manna, which neither you nor
your ancestors had known, to teach you that man does not live on
bread alone but on every word that comes from the mouth of
the LORD."

(Jesus quoted that verse during His own testing. It is a vital
principle to learn, which makes this one of the most visited wilderness
stops.)

So, God caused Israel to hunger, and then He fed them with supernatural food. In other words, He exposed their weakness – allowed them to feel the depth of their need – *and then* He showed them how willing and able He was to meet that need. He showed them how incapable they were of helping themselves *so that* they would recognise His ability and learn to value and depend on His loving-kindness for all they needed.

When we are in the wilderness, being faced with our own weakness does not feel like a kindness, does it? We feel broken, useless, desperate. Nobody likes to feel a burden – we all want to feel we bring more value to people than we take. But this is a very natural matter of human pride. And that gives us a hint of why humbling is so important.

In Proverbs 11:2 we see that humility is the opposite of pride: "When pride comes, then comes disgrace, but with humility comes wisdom."

Simply put, pride leads to destruction.[106] So humbling is not meant to be a cruelty but to save us from disgrace and destruction. Pride is both more insidious and more deeply dangerous than we realise. When we give in to that natural inclination to protect our own sense of value – to be self-sufficient and a positive contributor to society, we have exalted ourselves on the throne of our lives. Self rules. Self-image, self-respect, self-reliance, self-consciousness. It all sounds reasonable but can be so dangerous. It is selfish pride, which is idolatry.

There is a quirk in the English language where pride can have two meanings (at least). If I tell a friend or child that I am proud of them in a way that celebrates *their* efforts/achievements, I do not believe that is a problem. The pride that destroys is the kind of pride that takes the credit for their, or my own achievement. Or that insists I put in the effort to make myself better. It is considering self before God.

God wanting us to depend on Him is not a power trip. It is a blessing, because He knows He is the only source of the love, kindness, and every good thing we need for Kingdom life. Ever since the Fall we have been unable to be holy by ourselves. If we depend on ourselves,

---

[106] Proverbs 16:18

our best attempts at righteousness are like filthy rags.[107] We MUST learn to depend on Him, otherwise we would be devoid of hope and all things good. So, He humbles us to teach us dependence in certain areas, so we may apply it to our whole lives. It is His gift for life.

God humbles us by leading us into the wilderness to teach us that our blessings or success in life have nothing to do with us. This is particularly important for those of us who are naturally self-disciplined. For example, I am an organiser and a morning person, so it's not too hard for me to get up early and pray, or to keep up certain routines. But for others in my family, it does not come naturally at all – it is a real struggle. Does that make me better than them? Not at all – our brains are just wired very differently. But can it be tempting for me to judge them for not being as disciplined as me? Sadly, yes. So, God takes me into the wilderness (sometimes even stripping me of my normally easy regular early prayer times) to teach me that all my prayer life 'righteousness' does not make me any better than anyone else. It is a gift He has blessed me with, which reminds me I am still just as weak and needy of His grace as everyone else.

I do not like it. I hate feeling so dependent on anyone else, even Him – but that self-reliant pride must die, the same as all the areas of pride where we struggle. And we can be grateful for that humbling in the wilderness because the more we learn to lean on Jesus, the further we travel from destruction. And that is the ultimate kindness of God.

---

[107] Isaiah 64:6

Chapter 24 – Place of PREPARATION

*"And the child grew and became strong in spirit, and he lived
in the wilderness until he appeared publicly to Israel."*
Luke 1:80

O F ALL THE Bible characters we associate with the wilderness,
surely John the Baptist is one of those most likely to come to
mind? This wild man wearing camel-skin clothes and living
on a diet of locusts and wild honey[108] is synonymous with wilderness
living. He didn't just visit there from time to time – he grew up there!
I try to imagine what it must have been like to live there permanently,
and wonder how old he was when he left home and embraced the
desert. We know his mum and dad were both elderly when he was
born, so it is not a huge stretch to imagine that he could have been
bereaved of his parents and required to fend for himself at an early age.

But it was not just the presumed loss of his parents that would have
placed him there. At whatever age he was orphaned, prophet John was
clearly called to wilderness living, as we know from prophecy,[109] so he
was destined to spend significant time there in preparation. In fact, it
was a popular place of preparation for many of God's people – so if we
find ourselves in a similar season today, we can take courage that we are
in good company.

---

[108] Matthew 3:4
[109] Isaiah 40:3

Consider Moses, the prince of Egypt, who spent forty years as a shepherd in the wilderness. No doubt the humility and reliance on God that he learned there came in very handy when the time came to lead his whole nation through another forty years in the desert.

Joshua also learned to lead in the wilderness – as Moses' assistant, he would linger in the presence of God even after Moses had left.[110] There he learned to value God's voice and leading more than anything else – which became invaluable when Moses died and left him in charge.

Then there's David, whose youth was spent taking care of his father's sheep in the wilderness, where he learned the skills needed to kill lions and bears – skills that were very useful when Goliath came on the scene and everyone else was too scared to face him.

Even Jesus spent time in the wilderness, learning to resist the temptation to serve self – which would equip Him with the strength needed to pray, 'Not my will, but Yours be done,' in Gethsemane.[111]

And the apostle Paul, who would go on to write a third of the New Testament, also spent a time of preparation in the wilderness. Immediately after receiving Christ as his Lord and Saviour, he went to Arabia for three years. He said he was taught the gospel not by the apostles of Christ but by Jesus Himself,[112] which must have been during his time there, because after that he began his prolific ministry.

When we go through wilderness seasons, we rarely know what it is we are learning or being prepared for. It is not like school, where our lessons are clearly separated into subjects. Here we learn a multitude of strengths such as patience, hope, humility, and dependency on God. But imagine if God told us exactly what we were here to learn. We who are so used to learning academically, filling our heads with facts and 'Five steps to success in…', would spend a few days trying to identify the lesson and then declare that we had it and God could let us go home now! But the kind of lessons we learn here are less about head-knowledge, and more about character-training. And that takes a lot longer to

---

[110] Exodus 33:11
[111] Luke 22:42
[112] Galatians 1:11-18

develop. We cannot learn it academically: we must submit to the training, and that often requires repetition and perseverance until it becomes ingrained.

That's why sometimes we feel like we are repeating the same lesson over and over again. Perhaps God keeps talking to us about patience, or forgiveness, or trust (a few of the classic wilderness lessons). It is not because we are stupid or have failed or anything else we could be hard on ourselves about. It's just that as a good teacher, God knows it takes repetition to really develop a skill.

I doubt David was able to kill a lion with a single sling shot on day one of shepherding – most likely his first attempts were messy, painful, and exhausting. And, if Joshua had only spent a day in the presence of God hearing His voice, he might have written it off as a one-time experience and buckled under the pressure of leading. No, the confidence he later showed in receiving God's guidance could only have come from repeated practice. Even Paul, with all the training in the Law he had received in his younger days that made him a head Pharisee, still needed three years in the wilderness to learn the gospel to the depth that would be required for him to teach it.

And as for John the Baptist, he lived in the desert for so long it became his identity. Living only on what could be found there, he became a living example of the spiritual state of Israel: desperately dry and in need of living water. And so, his wilderness preparation became the preparation of Israel as he called them to repentance. And the message he preached resonated so strongly with those who acknowledged their desperate state that they were baptised into preparation right there in the desert, their hearts newly open and ready for Jesus, who would bring living water to quench their spiritual thirst.

So, we may not know what we are being prepared for – or how – but we can trust that when this wilderness season is over, we will be changed, equipped for whatever God has planned next. And it is going to be good!

Chapter 25 – Place of FEAR

"Do not be afraid, you wild animals, for the pastures in the wilderness are becoming green. The trees are bearing their fruit; the fig tree and the vine yield their riches."
Joel 2:22

THE IMAGERY IN today's verse is almost tangible. It speaks to the animals who live in the wilderness, assuring them that green pastures are coming again. But animals don't have the ability to reason and remember that life consists of seasons;[113] that dry seasons are always followed by seasons of plenty, as surely as spring follows winter. So, this encouragement does not just apply to animals – it is aimed at all who find themselves dwelling in the desert for a season. Because when we find ourselves in a dry and barren land, starved of food, it is hard to imagine ever finding food again. The very natural ongoing fear is that we are going to die of starvation there.

And when it comes to spiritual wildernesses, the fear experienced there can be even worse. When everything that our faith depends on is stripped away, our Bible reading feels dry and irrelevant, and our prayers seem pointless and ineffective as we are not sure anyone's even listening. When our efforts are bearing no fruit and we have no sense of God's presence or goodness with us, all hope is gone. And faith depends on hope.[114] Without hope, our faith falters: is God really

---

there? Has He abandoned me? What if I have got it all wrong? Have I wasted my life believing in a lie?

For me there is no fear that comes close to the fear of a life without God.

In my current wilderness season this has on occasion been a real concern. I have journeyed with God for long enough and seen His faithfulness often enough that I do not *think* my faith is really at risk. However, we are in a situation where we are at a complete dead-end. There is no natural way out. If God does not provide a miracle, I have no idea how we are going to get through. Now, I believe He has spoken many promises to me, from the Bible, through other Christians, and directly to me. I am putting my hope in Him and His Word. But still the risk is there: what if we do not receive those promises? Does it mean He is not there after all, and I have been deluded all along? Or does it mean He is still real, but everything I thought was true about our relationship and the way He speaks to me is *not* true? To be honest, I don't think one is easier to stomach than the other. It does feel like the very foundation of my faith is at risk. As I said to God this morning, I feel like I am playing 'chicken' with the devil: who is going to blink, or swerve, first? If I don't swerve, am I going to crash, leaving my faith destroyed? I have known God almost all my life – the thought of Him not being there is unbearable.

BUT… He has never let me down before. And I do not believe He is going to start now. I just need to cling to Him through the storm: to keep my eyes fixed on Him and not on the waves of fear being whipped up by the wind of pressures around me.

It is said there are 365 'fear nots' in the Bible – one for every day of the year. I suspect that's because God knew fear would be a daily temptation for as long as we live on earth, and He wanted us to know that whenever we are tempted to fear, we do not have to give in to it.

I haven't personally counted all the 'fear nots', but I have noticed that with the majority of those I have read, the exhortation to not fear is accompanied by a reason not to fear. And those reasons usually focus on God:

- "Do not be afraid, for I am with you." (Genesis 26:24)

- "Do not be afraid of them; the LORD your God himself will fight for you." (Deuteronomy 3:22)

- "Do not fear, for I myself will help you." (Isaiah 41:14)

- "Do not fear, for I have redeemed you; I have summoned you by name; you are mine." (Isaiah 43:1)

- "My Spirit remains among you. Do not fear." (Haggai 2:5)

- "Do not be afraid… your prayer has been heard." (Luke 1:13)

I have fought this fight against fear before, and from experience I know that the more I look at it, the more it grips me and appears real. The best way I have found to deal with fear is to look away from it and fix my eyes instead upon Jesus, on whom my faith depends, from beginning to end.[115]

As God said to me before, *'Those who focus on their troubles will fall prey to fear, anxiety, and hopelessness. But that is not what I have in store for My people. My beloved ones who live in the world, you are all surrounded by the same darkness and troubles as the rest of the world,[116] but you are not of the world – you have a different focus.*

*'As the darkness increases, those who focus on **Me** will receive My light – My joy, faith, and hope. And those who receive My light will carry it and reflect it to those around them who so desperately need it.*

'Oh, beloved, these are not times for you to fear – the temptation is all around you, but I have made a way to overcome. I AM the Way.[117] Keep your eyes on Me, and I will not let you fail.'

Amen!

---

[115] Hebrews 12:2
[116] John 16:33
[117] John 14:6

Many times through this wilderness I have felt strong reminders to keep my eyes fixed on Jesus. At times I have wondered why God keeps repeating Himself, but obviously I am still not getting it. I am so glad He is eternally patient and has promised to never let me go.

As things get dark around us, Christians must choose whether to focus on fear or to hope in Jesus. For the true disciples of Jesus will be made evident as the ones who hold joy and hope in the midst of a dying world. May that be us, Lord – may we keep our eyes fixed on You, and You alone. Amen.

Chapter 26 – Place of COMFORT

*"The L*ORD *will surely comfort Zion and will look with*
compassion on all her ruins;
he will make her deserts like Eden, her wastelands like the
*garden of the L*ORD.
Joy and gladness will be found in her, thanksgiving and the
sound of singing."
Isaiah 51:3

THIS VERSE IS one of my favourite hope-filled scriptures. We have been seeing how there are many blessings to be found in the wilderness, and hopefully as a result we are no longer railing against our season here. But nonetheless, the truth remains that this is a deeply uncomfortable, difficult place to be. So, this verse declaring that the wilderness *will* be comforted and restored to the beauty of Eden is a total blessing of hope. It is the biblical version of the saying 'this too shall pass'.

God's comfort here is more than just sympathy. Yes, His compassion is unfailing,[118] and He sympathises with us in our weakness and suffering.[119] But it goes even further: the word translated as 'comfort' is *nacham,* which carries a sense of completion – a comfort that ends the suffering. He does not just sympathise with our wilderness; He ultimately brings it to an end.

---

[118] Lamentations 3:22
[119] Hebrews 4:15

Friend, if you are in a dry season right now you can be reassured that He has not brought you here to leave you! This is not your final destination – it is a passing season that has a beautiful purpose. We can rarely see that purpose while we are surrounded by rocks and dust, but we can trust that God can. He sees the garden that is going to emerge out of our desert. He has promised to turn it into an Eden: the most perfect, beautiful, and alive dwelling place ever, where we will enjoy walking with Him.

I picture the wilderness as a dusty desert of dry soil and scree stretching as far as the eye can see, with dark, craggy mountains in the distance, a scorching sun high in the sky, and no trees anywhere for shade. Small prickly shrubs dot the landscape – no greenery, just sparse twiggy branches, and trip-hazard rocks scattered liberally everywhere. And of course, not a hint of water to be seen. It's so discouraging. Does your pictured wilderness look similar? They are always such painfully difficult places.

However, as I picture this right now, it is like God has expanded my vision to reveal something to us all. I look up from the dry and dusty ground and see someone in the distance waving. I want to escape this place, but he seems to be even further in, and I'm torn between trying to leave and wanting to meet this stranger. Starved of fellowship, I decide to push past my weakness to draw closer. Soon I see this man is dressed in white. Closer still, and he holds out a water bottle to me. I drink, and then as if dehydration were the only thing stopping me before, I begin to weep. He does not falter but draws me close and holds me even as I sink to the ground, not knowing whether I am crying from pain or relief. He kneels beside me, and I feel strength in his embrace. He produces bread for me to eat, and I feel stronger still. Then as I look up, he produces a trowel and a spade, and we start to dig. He seems to know exactly where to dig, and soon we have a hole filling with water. We drink together and rest a while, and then carry some water to pour over a few of the stunted shrubs. That night he stays with me – the darkness still pitch-black, but I am reassured by the sound of his breathing – and I sleep peacefully. The next morning, we awake and see grass growing around our pool. We turn to the watered shrubs and find leaves and fruit to sustain us. After we eat, he leads me to another area that we clear of rocks before starting to dig again. I blink, and time must have passed because now I see the desert has become a lush garden – this time green as far as the eye can see. The mountains in the distance now glow in the sun, and sparkling rivers run through the land, sheltered by trees bearing an abundance of fruit.

For me, this is a picture of the comfort of God. He does not just come to lend us a hanky or a shoulder to cry on – even though His are the most solid, eternally reliable shoulders we could ever lean upon – He comes to meet us in the desert, to turn our sorrow into joy, our weakness into strength, and our desert land into a garden. In Him is the fulfilment of the familiar verse where we make pools in the wilderness[120].

If, in my picture, I had been too focused on self-pity to look up or make myself respond, I would have suffered longer. If I had continued looking for an escape route and turned away from the man further in, I would have wandered for even longer. It was only in pushing ahead towards the man that I found what I needed. Sometimes when we encounter God in the wilderness, we treat Him like He is blaming us and unwilling to help or is just there to give us a drink and some food before we go back to trying to figure out how to manage by ourselves. But what if He does not want us to leave? What if this place is an area of our life that He wants to set up camp in and turn into a garden? To clear the rocks and water the feeble shrubs trying to grow? To deliver us from fear and shame, and cause rivers to spring up where all had been dry? To have us turn to Him for help in transforming what is lonely and dusty into something full of life and bearing fruit that will nourish others?

We all have dry wilderness areas inside our hearts that we cannot deal with by ourselves. But because of God's kindness and mercy, He does not overlook them but rather invites us to dwell there with Him and receive all He offers to turn the desolate land into a place of rich

---

[120] Psalm 84:6

blessing. He is the One who transforms our lives from deserts into Edens. So, when we come across these particularly dry places within, let's not dread them but rejoice, knowing He is about to work something beautiful in our hearts with the comfort that ultimately brings all dry seasons to an end.

Chapter 27 – Place of UNCERTAINTY

"The Lord had said to Abram, 'Go from your country,
your people and your father's family. Go to the land
I will show you.'...
Then Abram left and continued south toward
the Negev Desert."
Genesis 12:1,9 (NIRV)

ONE OF THE hardest things about wilderness seasons is the lack
of control we have. Unless we have deliberately chosen to
fast, we rarely have a say in when we enter, how long we will
be there, or what locations we will visit on the way. It is unknown, out
of our hands, and lacking in certainty – all of which makes it a fearful
place to be for us humans who like to try to control our lives.

It makes us realise how impressive it was for Abram to respond in
obedience when God called him to leave his country, relations, and all
that was comfortable in its familiarity to head to an unknown place.
God did not tell him where he was going, just that He would show it
to him as he went. So, Abram gathered his wife, nephew, and servants,
and headed into the unknown wilderness, trusting God to direct their
path as they travelled. What faith! Especially considering he – as far as
we can tell – was brand new to relationship with God. No wonder he
gained the title of Father of our faith!

Abram somehow knew the principle of God's faithfulness to lead us
that Isaiah later declared: "Though the Lord gave you adversity for

food and suffering for drink, he will still be with you to teach you…
Right behind you a voice will say, 'This is the way you should go,'
whether to the right or to the left."[121]

I experienced something like this a few years ago when I needed to
take my car for a drive to recharge its battery. As I started driving, I felt
God was inviting me to discover what it means to let Him be my
navigator. So, with plenty of fuel in the tank and no destination other
than eventually back home, I asked the Holy Spirit to be my guide and
lead me wherever He wanted.

That journey to unknown places was not exactly a wilderness (there
aren't many wildernesses here in England, and certainly none near my
home), but still, I was unfamiliar with much of it, so relying on God
to navigate required genuine trust as I tried to 'tune in' to His leading.
At the start of the journey, while I was still on familiar territory, I
found myself passing certain villages or hamlets whose names I
recognised. Pretty soon I was on unfamiliar roads but still recognising
the place names on the road signs. After a while we were on country
lanes with no more signs, and I was fully reliant on the Holy Spirit's
directions: approaching each junction I would ask, 'Which way?' and
wait for Him to lead me with His still small voice inside.

He led me along countless beautiful country lanes (I LOVE
country lanes, as God knows very well). The journey was incredibly
varied, from pretty countryside verges covered with multicoloured
wildflowers, through leafy-green tree tunnels in shady valley depths, to
high-up hilltops with glorious, far-reaching views. Never mind the
car's battery, it thoroughly recharged me!

On a couple of occasions I didn't hear and went the 'wrong' way:
once when I didn't notice a little signpost to a side turning until I drove
past it, and once when I came to a T-junction and chose my own
direction. On both occasions God immediately and lovingly corrected
me with an inner nudge and showed me a place to turn around.

Not long after we'd set off, I had vaguely thought I might like to
find a place I had driven through once before (and had loved for its

---

[121] Isaiah 30:20-21 NLT

spectacular views), but I could not remember how to get there. After following the Holy Spirit's leading through unknown places for some time, I noticed the name on a signpost, and I hoped we might be about to drive through it. However, closed roads, detours, and the continued prompting of God took me in a different direction. But as I passed the end of the detour and kept following the Holy Spirit, I found myself in that very place! I was overwhelmed by His kindness in surprising me with leading me to somewhere He knew I loved but couldn't reach by myself.

After I came through that place with the stunning views, I had to follow another detour around a road closure – and by the time I came to the end of it, I had absolutely no idea where I was or how to get home. I was still on the most remote of country lanes, with not a road sign to be seen. But God had stirred in me the spirit of adventuring through the unknown. At every junction I simply continued to ask, and He directed me. By now there was no stress or hesitation, just the peace and joy of journeying together until I found myself back on familiar roads heading home.

That drive with the Holy Spirit navigating was one of the most beautiful experiences of my life. Even more so because it happened during one of the Covid lockdowns, when we were all isolated and more uncertain than ever about what the future held. It was a very practical and tangible example of what it means to trust God with the unknown. I like to be in control and know where I am and where I am going – but when I experienced letting go of that and trusting God to guide me, He blessed me beyond what I thought was possible, both in the valleys and the high places of that journey. And later that day, as I reviewed my journey, I saw five clear lessons that God had taught me along the way, showing how even in uncertain times, we can trust Him:

- God knows us and knows how to bless us, even when we are on a practical mission.

- God will give encouraging signs and confirmations to those at the start of their journey, until we have been travelling with Him for long enough to be familiar with His voice and able to trust Him without needing any signs.

- God is bigger than any mistake! He does not lecture, criticise, or judge harshly, just points it out and graciously provides opportunity to head back in the right direction.

- God can and will use circumstances beyond our control to get us to the place of blessing where we are meant to be.

- God is well able to lead us, even when we have no idea where we are. The more we trust in His ability to lead us, the less stressful and the more peaceful it can be.

So, even though the wilderness remains an uncomfortable and uncertain place, sometimes we need to let go of control so we can learn how truly trustworthy God is to lead us and how much He loves to bless us. We can even relax about our mistakes and worldly obstacles because God is bigger than them all. We may not be able to see where we are going yet, but we can trust God's process. We *are* on the way. We are like Abram: only just left Haran, with packed bags loaded onto donkeys or camels, but without a map. No handy printout of directions to follow, no app showing every step of the way. Our destination may be uncertain to us, but God knows exactly where – and who – He wants us to be. So, let's trust Him with the navigation, obeying His leading one step at a time.

"Commit your way to the Lord,
Trust also in Him, and He shall bring it to pass."[122]

---

[122] Psalm 37:5 NKJV

Chapter 28 – Place of REFUGE

"Oh, that I had wings like a dove; then I would
fly away and rest!
I would fly far away to the quiet of the wilderness.
How quickly I would escape – far from this
wild storm of hatred."
Psalm 55:6-8 (NLT)

WHEN ISRAEL FIRST fled to the wilderness, they had little choice about it: the Egyptians they had just escaped were pursuing them again, to drag them back to captivity or worse.[123] Their only alternative was to trust the miraculous but terrifying (only slightly less terrifying than the Egyptians) path that had opened in front of them, leading into the desert. It was their first encounter with the truth that the wilderness is an ideal place for refuge: quiet, and far from everyday enemies. It is not that there are no enemies there, just that those who do make it that far are typically easy to spot coming from a long way off. Mostly, they avoid the discomfort there as much as everyone else.

When David wrote the psalm quoted in our opening verses, he was experiencing persecution from an enemy… again. Trembling with fear and longing for relief, he first prayed that God would not hide Himself or ignore his prayers[124] and then expressed his deep terror,

---

[123] Exodus 14:10
[124] Psalm 55:1

remembering in contrast the refuge of the wilderness. Although he had experienced lions and bears in the desert as a young lad and was later pursued there by a king bent on destroying him, to David it was a place associated most with peace and safety. Even if he picked up wounds in the process of fighting off a wild animal, the wilderness was his place of quiet that gave him time and space to heal before the next attack. But when he was king, the attacks – often from his own people – came thick and fast, without space to take a breath. Sometimes the enemy launches attacks like that at us too, and we receive multiple wounds in a short space of time.

The sad fact about life on this planet is that it is full of imperfect people. We ourselves are imperfect, and so are those around us – even those we love the most. And imperfect people invariably hurt others at some point, whether they mean to or not. Personally, I believe most people do not mean to be hurtful, but still it happens, just as we ourselves hurt people without intending to. And sometimes we go through seasons where that pain just seems to pile up, and we cry out for a break from the relentlessness of it all.

David experienced active hostility for most of his adult life. If it was not Saul pursuing him, it was another army. And once he was crowned king over all Israel, his own son revolted against him, wanting to seize the throne.[125] No wonder David longed for the simple peace of the wilderness. There might not be the rich comfort of palaces there, but he longed for the quiet, freedom, and space to recover in the deserts of his youth, when his only enemies were an occasional lion or bear.

Even when we are not actively hated by human enemies, as David was, many of us go through seasons where those around us seem to drag us down, or at least let us down. When we are weak or suffering and in need of friends who can lift us and stand with us, it can feel like hostility when we find no help from those around us. And worse still, when we cry out for help and end up like Job, surrounded with supposed 'friends' who just make things worse by blaming us for our

---

[125] 2 Samuel 15:10-14

suffering,[126] it truly adds insult to injury. I suspect Job would have liked to flee from his so-called friends into the wilderness, far from their 'helpful' (not) words!

Sometimes when we are seeking counsel, those who try to give good advice can make things worse. I had an experience where I was struggling with a situation and could not discern God's leading in it. I cried out to Him to send help, and then reached out to a few friends around me, asking for prayer and insight. To the best of my knowledge, they all prayed for me, which was invaluable and gave me real strength. I will always be grateful for the prayers of others. However, I also received conflicting advice from some of them, each saying they felt they had received it in prayer (they each also said to test it, so there was no arrogance there). I had to take it all to God to sift through and learn for myself what was from Him and what was from a different source. I became even more confused than when I started – through the conflicting voices of others.

I did not blame any of them for any error in their listening/advice, but I did realise that I was trying to short-circuit the reason I was in the wilderness: to hear God more clearly for myself. When we come to this place we need to embrace the element of refuge – relief from the many voices, opinions, wounds, and even sometimes attacks found in our everyday lives. It is a hard place to be, especially when we are there for a prolonged season – the loneliness mentioned in Chapter 11 can feel unbearable at times. But then we must remember that we are learning to depend on Jesus, and actually the silence and solitude of the wilderness is a blessing and a refuge: a place where our only companion – God – is entirely on our side and wanting to free us from the pain and confusion involved with other humans; to remind us that HE is our ever-present refuge.[127]

For when we learn this lesson, we will be better equipped to deal with the wounds that come from living among imperfect people. When we know the reality of God as our refuge, we won't have to travel

---

[126] Job 42:7
[127] Psalm 46:1

through the wilderness every time somebody hurts us, but we will be able to go straight to Him for refuge from the attacks of our true enemy, and for comfort and healing of wounds until we are strong again.

Chapter 29 – Place of DARKNESS

"Even though I walk through the darkest valley,
I will fear no evil, for you are with me;
your rod and your staff, they comfort me."
Psalm 23:4

ALTHOUGH THIS VERSE does not specifically mention a wilderness, it does speak of the *darkest valley*. And the truth is that shepherds and sheep, like those in this psalm, lived in the wilderness – it was where they moved around looking for grazing spaces. Sometimes, to get from one patch of food to another, they had to pass through deep ravines: narrow, constricted valleys of deep discomfort and darkness where they could not see what was ahead. And one of the worst things with such deep valleys is that we know there is light somewhere overhead, where others are walking in the bright blessings of sunlight. When we are lacking that light, somehow knowing what we are missing makes it an even lonelier, scarier, and darker place to be.

The valley here in Psalm 23 is the darkest one of all. Depending on your Bible version it might be translated as 'valley of the shadow of death', 'death-dark ravines', 'a valley as dark as the grave', 'the deepest darkness', or 'Death Valley'. Some scholars believe this latter Death Valley was a geographical place in the wilderness of Israel where children were sacrificed, fires burned perpetually, and danger lurked around every bend. Some believe it is a metaphor for the condition of life: that we are all mortal beings, gradually dying as we spend this brief but challenging time on earth until we pass over to a bright and beautiful eternal life with Jesus. Others apply it to the most difficult periods of life on earth – the troubles that come to us all at some point.[128] Whether we take it to be a literal or metaphorical valley, you get the point: this 'darkest valley' is the most scary, difficult, and lonely place to be. For in deep darkness, we cannot see anyone or anything – we are just aware of ourselves and our own discomfort and fear.

I have had a few dark seasons. When I lost two of my babies through miscarriage, when I moved to a place where I knew no one and didn't know why God had called me there (causing me to doubt if He *had* called me there), and when my dad died – these were the most dark, difficult, and painful seasons of my life. There were people around me – friends and family who prayed and offered what help they could – but the pain in my heart was so intense, and my ability to see anything so overshadowed by grief, nobody could really do anything to heal me. That privilege always belongs to God. He absolutely works through loved ones and counsellors as His hands and feet, to express love and comfort as much as humanly possible. But where the humanly-possible runs out, that is where the comfort of this verse really kicks in. In the darkest valley where no light can reach to show us the way ahead, even when we cannot see a thing, He is still with us.

I know there will be people reading this chapter who have been bereaved. There will be others who struggle with depression or terminal illness (for more on depression, please see Chapter 39). There will be many in dark valleys that I have little experience of. Whoever you are, and whatever your valley, my heart goes out to you. I pray you will experience the presence of God with you as you read this chapter and know He is with you right now.

When David wrote Psalm 23, I am sure he was remembering his own experience as a shepherd and the way he protected his flock with his life. Constantly vigilant, he would have used a rod (like a thick

---

[128] John 16:33

club) to protect his sheep from predators such as lions and bears,[129] and a longer, thinner staff (like a walking stick) to guide his sheep, nudging them in the right direction and steering them away from danger. When he led his flock, they would have been entirely reliant on him to know where he was taking them. And as sheep are not the smartest animals, David knew it was his sole responsibility to get them safely to their destination.

How much more do we, when travelling through the dark valleys that come to us all, need to place our trust entirely in our Good Shepherd to know where He is taking us and to be able to get us there safely, protecting and guiding us as we travel.

In truth, we have no need to fear, because the Lord Himself is our ever-present protection. Even when we go through dark and painful experiences, we are not alone. Jesus went through every sorrow we would ever face, so that we never have to be alone in them. When we are bereaved, He knows what that is like (He lived through the death of His earthly father and His cousin John, just for starters) – He meets us there. When we are sick, in pain, or dying, He experienced that too (death on the cross being the most brutal way to die) – He meets us there. When we are mentally and emotionally tormented, He understands[130] – He meets us there. When we are rejected and let down by friends or persecuted by enemies, He has been through it all – He meets us there. And He who experienced it all also overcame it all and has been raised to victorious eternal life. He is here with us now, nudging us along with His staff of direction and using His rod to protect us from the enemy who seeks to destroy.

That is why we need fear no evil: even in seasons when it's too dark to see anything, there is nothing that man or the devil can do to us that has the power to take us out of Jesus' hands. For He is WITH US. He has travelled this dark valley before and knows the way that leads us out. Only He protects us from being destroyed by or lost in the darkness – if we stick close to the shepherd and trust Him to lead us

---

[129] 1 Samuel 17:34
[130] Luke 22:44

out, He keeps our eternal souls safe. He meets us there, not just in a sympathetic fellowship-of-suffering way – although that alone is inexpressibly comforting – but in a hope-filled, overcoming, *'I have been there too so I can be with you in it, then lead you to eternal victory with me'* kind of way.

So, though we may walk through the darkest valley, we need fear no evil. For He is with us here in the valley, and He is leading us to green pastures. Anyone who learned about photosynthesis at school will know that green plants need sunlight to grow. So, we know we will come out into the light again – it is a promise, made by our Good Shepherd.

Chapter 30 – Place of HOLINESS

*"Water will gush forth in the wilderness and
streams in the desert…
And a highway will be there; it will be called
the Way of Holiness."*
Isaiah 35: 6,8

HOLINESS IS SUCH a misunderstood term sometimes: it conjures up haloed images of impossibly pious, spiritually perfect individuals, far out of reach of the rest of us who are still struggling with our complicated earthly lives. God is holy, the angels are holy, the saints of old in Heaven are holy… but us? We are a mess! And yet God has called us to be holy[131] – so how is that even possible? Well, on our own it is not, but thankfully we are not on our own. The sin that makes us such a complicated mess is the very reason Jesus came to earth: to save us from its power and restore us to holiness.

Because holiness simply means to be 'set apart'. It means to be different from everyone else, dedicated to God. No haloes required. We can dedicate our lives to God even while our lives are imperfect because Jesus has made the way. He was holy: His whole life was set apart and dedicated to God. And when He died for us, He made the way for all who believed in Him and received His perfect sacrifice on our behalf to be made perfect in Him. Our lives may not be perfect, but if we are in Christ, we are perfect in God's sight.

---

131 1 Peter 1:16

And yet the curious thing is, although God accepts us as perfect through Christ, He does not have blinkers on. He can still see all the imperfections in our lives and works to help us overcome them in a process called sanctification, where we who choose it become gradually more holy – allowing His holiness to displace our sinful tendencies – every day.

But it is not a passive, or even an automatic process. While we live on earth, we live in a body of physical flesh surrounded by an ungodly environment ruled over by an enemy – all of which continuously tempt us to choose our own way over God's way. Everything naturally in and around us fights against God's sanctification process. And for those of us in the West, our biggest enemies are the distractions of comfort and busyness. In our comfortable homes with our busy, distracted lives, who has time to fully commit to being set apart for God? We focus on our families, paying the bills, trying to do our jobs well, caring for those we are responsible for, and if we get time to rest, we fill it with all the many distractions available: sports, movies, pubs, social media, TV etc. God often comes a long way down the list. So, He allows wilderness seasons to clear our agendas and turn our focus back to Him. For it is here that we are faced with the choice: am I going to whine like the Israelites, longing to get my old life back, or am I going to choose God's way?

Our opening verses speak about the "highway of holiness" formed in the wilderness. A highway is a raised-up road, free from rocks and obstacles that would hinder a journey. Wouldn't we all love an easy road out of this place? Well, the truth is, there is a way available, but it is only found through holiness. The road that leads out of the wilderness appears when we surrender our own will and desires to God and seek for our lives to be more fully set apart and devoted to Him. That is the holiness developed through sanctification: the process that demands we daily crucify our 'self' – our own needs and desires – to pursue and obey the leading of the Holy Spirit.

Naturally speaking, very few of us *want* to spend time praying, studying, fasting, tithing, preaching the gospel and so on: it is all deeply uncomfortable to our self-centred, comfort-seeking flesh. But all those things require us to deny self. They do not automatically make us holy in themselves, but the more we use them to express our hearts' desires to be more like Jesus, and the more we devote our lives to learning how to be like Him, the more set apart we will become.

In the wilderness we must confront our own selfishness and take the opportunity to choose a better way. Here we are faced with our emptiness apart from God; we see the meaninglessness of much of what we fill our lives with, and we are invited to pursue what is more eternally important.

Because holiness is not a prison – it is freedom. Freedom from sin, suffering, and eternal separation from God. And it is power: for the more set apart we become, the more space we make inside for Jesus to be formed in us; the more surrendered we are to God's will in us, the more He will be able to work in us to bless us and those around us. What feels uncomfortable to our souls is the very breath of God to our spirits. It is not about God forcing us into discomfort and death – it is about Him wanting us to find abundant life.

When we became Christians and entered the covenant that exchanged our sin for Jesus' life, God took that exchange seriously. He longs for us to be set free from all the selfish ways we are used to, because He knows we will be so much happier and more fulfilled; more like Him (and who does not want that?). He wants us to walk in the fullness of HIS Kingdom, not the harsh and constricting kingdom of this world, however appealing it seems.

But the choice is always ours, whether to continue on the path to eternal life or to go back and satisfy our self-seeking in this life. And like we saw in Chapter 1 about the place of tempting: when we are in an uncomfortable place, the enemy loves to make the comfortable familiarity of this fallen world and our own sinful selfishness seem really appealing. But if we take the opportunity to fix our eyes on Jesus and the fullness and freedom of a life lived in and for Him, we will take the highway of holiness that leads out of the wilderness and all the way to a glorious eternity with God.

Chapter 31 – Place of SUFFERING

"I have refined you in the furnace of suffering."
Isaiah 48:10 (NLT)

IN THIS CHAPTER we are going to look at something that we all associate with the wilderness, and then some. It is like the wilderness on steroids: where a desert is known to be dry, hot, and uncomfortable, multiply that several times over and we find ourselves in a furnace, with its unbearable heat. That is suffering.

It is a difficult subject to cover, as it taps into the great questions that even theologians throughout the years have tried and failed to fully comprehend: if God is real, good, and kind, why is there so much suffering in the world? We know that God is not the One who causes suffering – it is Satan who comes to steal, kill, and destroy, while Jesus came to give us life in abundance,[132] and it is clear which of those camps suffering belongs to. And yet, God allows it to continue. In part that's because we live in a fallen world – for as long as this world remains, we will have trouble[133] – and it is only when this world is ended and we step into eternity with Jesus that every tear will be wiped away and there will be no more death, mourning, crying, or pain.[134] But still we wonder *why* God allows His precious loved ones to suffer. We know He is our loving Father who wants to bless us, and we know any good parent would do anything to protect their child from pain if

---

[132] John 10:10
[133] John 16:33
[134] Revelation 21:4

possible. But when we read verses like our opening one from Isaiah, it sounds like God has endorsed the path of pain and suffering for us. Why would He do that?

Here He says it is for refining.

Ouch – sounds deeply uncomfortable! Refining a precious metal goes deeper than the testing of Chapter 21. It must be heated until it is liquefied, so the dross and impurities can rise to the surface and be skimmed off, leaving the metal in a purer state. It is an extreme process. If we apply that concept to our own lives, we can be thankful that we are not literally liquefied, but still: refining does not feel nice or comfortable. It involves intense 'heat' in our lives and a rising to the surface of contaminants hidden deep within we would rather not have to look at. Being in God's furnace can result in old issues cropping up in our lives that we thought we had already conquered. So, the purification process requires us to not suppress fresh conviction over areas of compromise or write them off as insignificant, or try to move on in our own strength, but to lean in with that famous prayer from the psalms:

"Search me, God, and know my heart; test me and know my anxious thoughts. See if there is any offensive way in me, and lead me in the way everlasting."[135]

In that way, as the impurities rise to the surface, we can take them straight to God who is the only One able to fully deal with them.

And remember that the purification process builds on God's testing: when He allows the heat of affliction to bring hidden impurities to the surface, it is not so He can judge if we pass or fail His standards: it is to identify and remove whatever is not of Him, so we can be commissioned by Him as His proven holy vessels, carriers of His pure light.

Suffering is a deeply personal and holy matter. Jesus was called a "man of suffering, and familiar with pain".[136] By taking on physical human form, He deliberately exposed Himself to the condition of

---

[135] Psalm 139:23-24
[136] Isaiah 53:3

decay and gradual death each one of us has been subject to since the Fall. And of course, through His physical suffering in the wilderness, in the Garden of Gethsemane, through His scourging and crucifixion, He experienced more suffering than we can imagine. So, when we suffer physical pain and weakness, we know He has gone before so He can meet us there.

There are of course other examples of suffering in the Bible. Recently I have been inspired and comforted by the examples of Shadrach, Meshach, and Abednego – persecuted and thrown into a literal furnace for their own refusal to turn their backs on God.[137] They trusted God to save them but declared they would not reject Him even if He allowed them to suffer and be destroyed (purity revealed by the furnace, right there!). In my current wilderness/furnace season, I feel I have caught a glimpse of this, though obviously nowhere near as extreme as their experience…

After a lifetime of relationship with a faithful God, when He recently seemed to break His promise to me it was painful. I didn't suffer physically, but emotionally it was a harrowing ordeal. The pain and confusion left me questioning whether God was who I thought He was. It felt like my whole faith and future relationship with Him was under threat. Would He step in and prove Himself for me? Or would I die without Him? The heat and pressure in this place were painfully intense. But as I eventually emerged out of the other side of the furnace, God showed me that this suffering had been for a purpose.

In the furnace of suffering, I realised that when God did not 'keep His promise' (or do what I thought He should), I was loving Him for what He did for me rather than purely for who He is. And as that dross rose to the surface, I was able to cry out for a grace like Shadrach, Meshach, and Abednego, to worship Him whatever He does, just because He is God and He is good – and that will always be true, whatever I go through. As I emerged from the furnace, God revealed that he had burned away the dross and left me with a heart of purer

---

[137] Daniel 3:4-21

worship. That discovery was like finding pure gold. The refining had been worth it. It always is.

The truth is, He never leaves us to be destroyed. As the oppressor Nebuchadnezzar witnessed, Shadrach, Meshach, and Abednego were joined in the fire by a fourth man who looked "like a son of the gods".[138] Scholars tend to agree this was a Christophany: an appearance of Jesus Christ at a time outside of His physical life on earth. Jesus was so concerned with His servants' suffering that He appeared in person to save them. They still had to pass through the furnace, but He was with them to overcome.

So, when we pass through the furnace of suffering, we may not be able to answer all the questions that arise about why God has allowed our particular affliction. But we can be reassured that it is never wasted. He is using it to refine us and purify our faith. We can take courage knowing we are not alone: Jesus – who endured the worst suffering known to man – stands with us in the fire. He will not leave us alone to be destroyed but will prove to be our very closest companion.

For God Himself has promised, "When you walk through the fire, you will not be burned; the flames will not set you ablaze. For I am the Lord your God, the Holy One of Israel, your Saviour."[139]

---

[138] Daniel 3:25
[139] Isaiah 43:2-3

Chapter 32 – Place of GOD'S GLORIOUS PRESENCE

*"While Aaron was speaking to the whole Israelite community,
they looked toward the desert, and there was the glory of
the Lord appearing in the cloud."*
Exodus 16:10

OR ALL THAT is dry, lonely, dark, and desperate about the wilderness, we cannot ignore the fact that in the Bible it is clearly a place where God loves to reveal His glory.

God's glory – the word *kabowd* – is another way of describing His manifest presence, which is when His presence is seen or felt with our physical senses. In the case of our opening verse, it was a shining glory, visible within a cloud. The cloud was a necessary cloak because if Israel had looked upon His pure glory, it would have killed them all – no human can withstand that level of holiness. But nonetheless, God wanted to be seen. He remained visible for the entire forty years of Israel's wandering – a constant presence, whether in cloud or fire, reminding them they were not alone. And it was not even just the pillar of cloud – there were the times when God's glory rested on Mount Sinai[140] and when the mountain smoked and shook with thunder, lightning, and trumpet blasts, and fire fell as God revealed His presence right there in the middle of them all.[141]

---

[140] Exodus 24:16
[141] Exodus 19:16-19

And yet despite all these miraculous and unmissable manifestations of God's presence with Israel, they still overlooked it. They still grumbled and complained about being in the wilderness, railing against Moses and longing to return to slavery in Egypt because it was what they knew and were familiar with.

We tend to think that if God appeared to us in His glory, our lives would be changed. But so often in the Bible we see His glory is mainly revealed in the wilderness. How many people are willing to leave the comfort of their everyday lives to venture into the desert in the hope of a glimpse of God's glory? I suppose anyone fasting right now could be one of those people, for when we fast, we deliberately deprive ourselves of what is normal, comfortable, and familiar, in order to seek God. But even if we're in a season that we entered reluctantly, like the Israelites – God still wants us to encounter His glory here. For there is something about the wilderness, where all else is hostile and uncomfortable, that helps us see so much more clearly the truth that God's presence is all we really need. And when we realise that, we are in the best position to recognise Him.

We must take care in these seasons that we do not spend so much time complaining about how hard it is here and desperately trying to leave that we miss the very presence of God right here with us. We may not be blessed with a pillar of cloud or fire in our living rooms, but we have something better: the Holy Spirit Himself living inside us, in all His glorious resurrection power. Even when the environment around us becomes dry, difficult, and hostile, His glory is still within. We just need to take our eyes off our circumstances and learn to look in the Spirit to find the deeper truth of His constant glory always with us.

As I believe God said when I asked Him about it, *'I am always with you, My child. My presence is always with you; My glory is always available to you. In the wilderness I allow you to become aware of your hunger and thirst for Me more than anything else, so that you will call out for My presence as the very air you need to breathe. And then I will answer. For I long to reveal My glory to you. I long for you to experience My presence more deeply than any other worldly reality. You just need to ask –*

to value it above all your lesser treasures. And then, when you learn to look in the Spirit-realm, you will see. Then you will grow in knowing Me as your spirit desires. My glory is not cheap, beloved: it is only those who value and pursue My presence who will truly see it.

'In the wilderness you learn that My presence is so much more than a few fleeting goosebumps: it is weighty, glorious, and constant. But it is available to you. I am available to you. I am with you in the fullness of My presence, if you will only search for Me with your whole heart,[142] *as desperately as one searches for water in the wilderness.'*

Amen.

---

[142] Jeremiah 29:13

Chapter 33 – Place of
SURROUNDING PRESSURES

*"After Saul returned from pursuing the Philistines, he was
told, 'David is in the Desert of En Gedi.' So Saul took three
thousand able young men from all Israel and set out to look for
David and his men near the Crags of the Wild Goats."*
1 Samuel 24:1-2

DAVID WAS IN a tight spot. And it was not his fault. He had
done nothing wrong – in fact, he had done everything right.
The first time we read of him in the Bible, he was a
teenager tending his father's sheep in the wilderness.[143] Secretly
anointed by Samuel to become king of Israel, David continued in
humility. He divided his time between shepherding his father's flocks
and serving in King Saul's court as an armour-bearer and musician,
playing the lyre to soothe Saul's troubled moods.[144] Then came Goliath
with all his taunts, and suddenly David rose to prominence as the only
person with the courage and faith in God to not only face the giant in
battle, but defeat him.[145] From that point on David's status as a mighty
warrior continued to grow – along with Saul's jealousy. Even though
David always acted honourably, continuing to faithfully serve the king
both as a warrior and a personal minister through music, Saul

---

[143] 1 Samuel 16:8-12
[144] 1 Samuel 16:21-23
[145] 1 Samuel 17:4-51

persecuted him and repeatedly attempted to kill him until David had to flee for his life, hiding in the desert. He spent the next ten years living there.

Just as we saw with Joseph, so we see here again with David: there are times in the lives of some of God's people when they find themselves in the wilderness through no fault of their own. Being here feels like punishment, and when it is accompanied by persecution or people misunderstanding us and accusing us of wrong, it can be tempting to either fall into self-pity (I don't deserve this) or questioning ourselves (*did* I do something wrong?). But David's example is another reminder to us that there is little point trying to understand how we came to be here, either to defend ourselves or condemn ourselves. We just need to focus on God and what He wants to show us.

David's desert experience came with extra pressures. As we have seen, most people in the wilderness experience it as an isolated, lonely time, but at times David had a different kind of hardship. Isolated from the love of his wife and his best friend, he was joined first by his parents and brothers with their households, seeking his protection. It rapidly escalated further when, "All those who were in distress or in debt or discontented gathered around him, and he became their commander. About four hundred men were with him."[146] David sent his parents to stay somewhere safer,[147] but it seems his brothers remained, so now David was responsible for the safety of several hundred unhappy, broke, and dysfunctional people. He knew how to look after himself in the wilderness: he had done so from an early age. But leading a tribe of discontents is a whole other burden. He was surrounded, not just by the persecution of the king of Israel, but by the complaints, distress, and needs of those around him, all struggling to survive and demanding that he lead the way.

Very few of us enter wilderness seasons with the luxury of only ourselves to manage. Most of us have family responsibilities – whether

---

[146] 1 Samuel 22:2
[147] 1 Samuel 22:3-4

families at home, church families, or both. We have jobs, neighbours, and so on. Nobody lives in a bubble – our lives are all interconnected, and it is meant to be that way, for community is at the heart of God's Kingdom. But when we enter a dry season, the sense of responsibility for others' wellbeing can make everything many times harder, especially when they have their own troubles too, which make us feel even more powerless.

Fast forward a few years, and David was still hiding in the wilderness, still being hunted by King Saul. His first wife had been taken from him and given to another, but he now had two more wives, and his desert army was growing. The women, children, and supplies were often left behind as David and his men went out, and at one point this happened at a place called Ziklag. But when David's army returned, they found that the Amalekites had raided their camp, taken all their loved ones, and burned what was left. Talk about discouragement! They all wept until they had no strength left to weep.[148] And then the men with him fully turned against him: "David was greatly distressed because the men were talking of stoning him; each one was bitter in spirit because of his sons and daughters."[149]

The anointing/promise that God had made all those years ago must have felt like a dream. But then – and I believe this is one of the reasons David was called a man after God's heart[150] – he did something that not only saved his life, but the lives of all his people, and would ultimately see him on the throne He was destined for: "But David found strength in the Lord his God."[151]

Imagine that! Was David particularly strong, to be able to encourage himself in this way? Or was he utterly desperate, at the end of all his strength, and simply knowing that only God could get him through? Personally, I think it was both: I think it does require a certain mental strength to call out to God instead of giving in to hopelessness – but all the strength was God's. David had been in the

---

[148] 1 Samuel 30:4
[149] 1 Samuel 30:6
[150] 1 Samuel 13:14, Acts 13:22
[151] 1 Samuel 30:6

wilderness a long time – he knew he had no strength of his own left; all that remained was God, so he called out to Him and received His strength.

I believe one good reason David was in the desert for so long was because he was learning to be more than a good shepherd and a mighty warrior: he was learning to be strong in the Lord, even when those he was leading turned against him. Just as we are told it is the pressure on a carbon deposit that turns it into a diamond (the hardest but also most beautiful substance known to humankind), so too does the pressure of multiple wilderness troubles bring out extra strength and beauty within us.

In my current season, I have found the pressure of numerous troubles to be particularly difficult: some troubles coming in the form of external pressures, and some coming from those who are close to me, not least because I feel responsible for helping them to navigate the wilderness too. I have prayed that God will teach me to strengthen myself as David did – that I would find the Lord's strength here and not let go. And in answer, God took me to some principles that deserve a chapter of their own. We will find them in tomorrow's reflections on strengthening…

Chapter 34 – Place of STRENGTHENING

"When David and his men reached Ziklag (in the Judean wilderness), they found it destroyed by fire and their wives and sons and daughters taken captive… David was greatly distressed because the men were talking of stoning him; each one was bitter in spirit because of his sons and daughters. But David found strength in the LORD his God."

1 Samuel 30:3,6

As I READ this account and asked God to teach me how to find His strength in the wilderness, I felt invited to look at some practical ways that David did so. Surrounded by the pressures of his wives and household being kidnapped by enemies, and both the king's army and now his own friends – all of whom he had only ever served faithfully – all trying to kill him, there was only One who could help him: God. David could have given in to the bitterness gripping his men. He could have descended into self-pity, whined about how unfair it was, and blamed God for letting him down and going back on His promises – but instead he looked to God for strength.

When all our prayers seem to be bouncing off the ceiling, all the promises we ever received have been delayed to the point of feeling like a malicious joke, and the enemy's hopelessness is trying to smother us, how do we imitate David and find strength in God? Thankfully, David left us some examples in his psalms – there are lessons there, and elsewhere in the Bible, which can help us once we decide to reject self-pity and bitterness and seek God for his strength. For example, Psalm 18:6 says, "In my distress I called to the Lord; I cried to my God for help."

I would suggest all desperate prayers boil down to this: 'Lord, help!' There is no shame in running out of our own strength or ability to cope – in fact, it is wisdom to recognise our own weakness and cry out for help from the One who promised He would always be with us. Our eternal Saviour and loving Father is ALWAYS ready to help and give us strength for the season we are in, if we ask Him.

Then there is Psalm 103:2: "Praise the Lord, my soul, and forget not all his benefits." That's two lessons in one verse:

1. Praise God. I've heard it said that the part of our brain that feels anxiety and the part that feels thankful cannot operate at the same time. David commanded his soul (the part of himself that felt desperate) to override his feelings and praise God. When we deliberately choose thankfulness, when we praise God for His goodness and faithfulness, we cannot focus on worries or discouraging circumstances. So, we choose to lift Him higher in our sight. Even when we feel so low that praising Him is an act of obedience rather than feeling (feelings are not as trustworthy as the truth), declaring His praise releases eternal truth that lifts our feelings above our circumstances. It is for this reason I have a playlist of 'rejoicing' songs and 'breakthrough' songs that avoid feeling-based lyrics and simply declare the jubilant truth of how wonderful God is. Sometimes we all need help to step out of feelings and into truth. And the Holy Spirit loves to help us once we choose.

2. Forget not His benefits – i.e. REMEMBER how He has shown love to us in the past. The other day I woke up and the faith I had been walking in seemed to have wavered. I felt

a bit down, and that nasty age-old question started to arise: 'Did God really say…?' I did not bother wasting time trying to deal with my feelings; I just asked God for help, and He led me to re-read my journals to remind myself of all the blessings He had faithfully given and all the answers to prayer I had received. When faith is challenged, we encourage ourselves by remembering His goodness, from our own journals and all the Bible stories that declare His faithfulness (e.g. Noah, Abraham, Isaac, Jacob, Joseph, Moses, Joshua, Rahab, Ruth, Samuel, David, Daniel, Deborah, Esther, and so on).

Another strengthening verse is Matthew 11:28: "Come to me, all you who are weary and burdened, and I will give you rest."

Jesus spoke these words a long time after David practised strengthening himself in God – but they continue the theme. He specifically invited us to exchange our burdens for His rest, because His compassion for us is endless.[152] Remember He was tempted as we are – He understands[153] and made a way for us to overcome. Hopelessness, weariness, desperation, doubts, fears – these are all burdens we are not meant to carry. On the cross, Jesus carried them all on our behalf, so we no longer must. So today, we can come to Him in prayer and tell Him (write it down if it helps) all the things that we struggle with – our doubts, fears, and temptations to unbelief – and then leave it with Him. We receive His compassion and strength and know He has dealt with all our problems and made a way for us to walk in the hope, joy, victory, and freedom of His Kingdom.

Finally (for this chapter – but do see which other strengthening verses you can also find), there is 1 Thessalonians 5:11: "Therefore, encourage one another and build each other up, just as in fact you are doing."

---

[152] Lamentations 3:22
[153] Hebrews 4:15

We are not often truly isolated… for long, at least. At Ziklag David was surrounded by enemies and hostile 'friends' – he felt more alone than ever and had to draw solely on God for His strength. And God met him there – as He always does with us when we are truly alone. But thankfully those times are few. Even when Elijah the prophet felt like he was the only faithful one left, he soon learned that God had reserved a remnant of faithful worshippers.[154] Not everyone will be on the same page as us all the time, but God does usually send people for mutual encouragement. If we can't think of any Christian friends like that, it is a good idea to ask Him to show us whom He has in mind – and then make time for each other, be vulnerable with each other, and pray together. In this season I have found so much blessing from being vulnerable and asking others for prayer support, whether praying together with friends or them remembering to pray for me in their own prayer times.

Even so, godly friends are no substitute for walking in friendship with the Holy Spirit – He wants to come first. But the friends who point us back to the Lord are still a gift to be treasured!

So, if you feel in a bit of a Ziklag wilderness season right now – the promises you once received seem far removed from your reality, those around you aren't helping, and you have no strength left to fight in faith – let me encourage you to find your strength in the Lord like David. It took about fifteen years after he received God's promise and anointing before he was finally crowned: sometimes there seem to be exhausting delays that we just do not understand. But God is still good. Always. So, we turn to Him for strength, and eventually we will see His breakthrough.

---

[154] 1 Kings 19:18

Chapter 35 – Place of THIRST

"I thirst for you, my whole being longs for you,
in a dry and parched land where there is no water."
Psalm 63:1

ONE OF THE most common associations with the wilderness is the sense of dryness. Just as we saw in Chapter 29 how darkness is the result of a lack of light, here we have a similar theme: dryness and thirst are the result of a lack of water.

David had been a shepherd – he knew how dry and uncomfortable the desert could be. He would have known what it was like to be desperately thirsty – the kind of thirst that comes from serious dehydration. When we are that thirsty, we are not able to focus on anything else except meeting that need.

In previous dry seasons I asked God how it is possible to experience dry wilderness seasons when He is in us: if we have Holy-Spirit rivers flowing from our inmost being,[155] how can we also feel dry and weary?

And I believe God showed me that sometimes our life's journey takes us through times of richness and blessing when we have plentiful supplies of water all around, e.g. the secure love of a close family, flourishing relationships with encouraging friends, and sound, Spirit-filled teaching from a good church community, as well as our own relationship with the Lord. But when our path takes us through wilderness seasons, some of those springs of water can seem to dry up:

---

[155] John 7:37-39

maybe family members have other needs or struggles, friends become distracted or disappear, church might become a place of offence. In these times, our only source of refreshing is our relationship with God. And suddenly we need to draw ALL our water from just that one well. The source never dried up; we just didn't have to rely on it quite so much before, so now, if there are any blockages to the flow (e.g. guilt, shame, pride, unforgiveness, hard-heartedness etc.), it becomes apparent far more quickly, leaving us desperately thirsty and fully aware that only He can help.

Sadly, it sometimes requires that level of desperation to provoke us to clear any blockages and dig deeper so we can drink from God's wellspring of living water.

It is said that some years of drought can be good for grapevines: although the stress on the plant causes them to produce less fruit, the grapes that do grow are much better quality, leading to more flavourful wine. And in vineyards with an abundant water table below ground, some vine growers choose to deliberately restrict irrigation because it forces the grapevines to send their roots much deeper to find water.[156]

It reminds me of Psalm 1:1-3, where the man whose delight is in God and His Word becomes "like a tree planted by streams of water, which yields its fruit in season and whose leaf does not wither".

Times of dryness and desperate thirst prompt us to put our roots down deeper – probing further into God's Word, seeking His Spirit, so we can access that living water more readily than we did before. Because we all have that source of living water flowing from within us, we need wilderness seasons to inspire us to respond to the conditions by sending down deep roots and intentionally drinking. And what helps us to flourish through a drought will bring even more abundant life in the greener seasons to come, with surplus fruit that will bless others too.

So, as I prayed from my place of desperate need I heard Him speak:

---

[156] Thanks to https://www.samsarawine.com/education/winemaking-in-times-of-drought/ June 29, 2022

'The season for rain *is* coming, beloved: have I not promised rivers in the wilderness, in the dry and deserted wastelands?'[157] I do not lie, and I do keep My promises. But right now, as the drought around you reaches desperate levels, I am calling you to put your roots down deeper than ever and drink of Me. Only My Spirit can satisfy; only My infilling can quench the thirst you carry from your season in the wilderness.

'The blessings I send sometimes give the illusion that you are drinking of Me, and as a result, My people can become dangerously spiritually dehydrated. In My mercy I temporarily remove those mirages so that all can come to see their true need to drink from their individual relationship with Me. Let all who are thirsty come to Me and drink!'[158]

It is always encouraging to be reminded that God keeps His promises and that the promised rivers in the desert *are* coming. Even when it doesn't feel like it, we can be sure God is never late: His timing is always perfect, and He knows what He is waiting for, so we can trust Him. Meanwhile, He allows us to feel frustration so we are driven to pursue Him, like Elijah declaring rain and then needing to pray repeatedly with childbirth-like intensity[159] until he saw the first sign of fulfilment.

It does feel like challenging work, especially when there is a drought all around us and it is a temptation to just drink enough to get by. But God is blessing us with the training to put down deep roots to be able to drink from the rivers of living water flowing through us in the Spirit at *all* times.

So, let's press into Him, put down deeper roots to drink more fully of Him, and be encouraged that this season is temporary: the promised next season is coming, and after a bit more patient endurance we *will* see it come to pass.[160]

---

[157] Isaiah 43:19
[158] John 7:37
[159] 1 Kings 18:42
[160] Galatians 6:9

Chapter 36 – Place of FOCUS

*"In those days John the Baptist came, preaching in the
wilderness of Judea and saying, 'Repent, for the kingdom of
heaven has come near.' This is he who was spoken of through
the prophet Isaiah: 'A voice of one calling in the wilderness,
"Prepare the way for the Lord, make straight paths for him."'"*
Matthew 3:1-3

THERE ARE FEW places that offer anything like a wilderness experience in England, but Dartmoor comes close. I went camping with a small group there once, on a trip that involved a hike across the moor followed by setting up camp, then a further hike the next morning to our final destination. One of the things that was impressed upon us as we prepared was not to try to carry any more than was absolutely necessary: each of us had one rucksack containing our tent, sleeping bag, food, waterproofs, and the minimum of other essentials such as a torch and compass. When we are navigating a wilderness, we learn very quickly that excess baggage will only wear us down. We must learn to discern what is superfluous and what is essential.

John the Baptist was a brilliant example of this. The wilderness was his home – he was not concerned with the comforts of 'civilised' living. Imagine all the places we have been exploring through this book, and then imagine making a home there. John was utterly used to a life of deprivation and discomfort: he lived a life permanently stripped back to the bare minimum with no distractions, so he could focus solely on God and what He was calling him to. He lived in that place of no worldly comfort so he could focus on what was spiritually important. It was a place of constant awareness that **nothing else matters**. And consequently, he was an uncomfortable person to be around: he didn't hold back from calling out the Pharisees for their dead religion; he didn't bring a nice fluffy message pandering to the people's sensitivities. He just called out, 'Repent! For the Kingdom of God is near!' because ultimately that was the bare-bones, stripped-back, focused message Israel needed to clearly hear.

When I have chosen to enter the wilderness by way of voluntarily undergoing a fast, it is usually for that reason: to strip back the superfluous fluff in my life (such as TV, social media, food treats, and other self-indulgent things) so that I can focus more on God, hearing His voice and catching His heart. Because often our comfortable western lives get in the way of what is important. Whether it be following a sports team, shopping, hobbies, or any other number of things we do purely for enjoyment, our culture makes it extremely easy to be distracted and not pay enough attention to God. Even going to church and filling our lives with busy activities there can rob us of the simple time to sit at His feet and talk with Him. These things are not necessarily wrong, but they can easily become a distraction.

Mary and Martha are a well-known example of this. The sisters both had the same guests to look after. But while Martha busied herself with all the practicalities of serving, Mary chose to lay them aside to be with Jesus. The Bible says Martha was *distracted,* drawn away by all the preparations that had to be made.[161] So she complained to Jesus, asking Him to make Mary help, but Jesus declared Mary had chosen the better approach.[162] Even hospitality, a fundamental principle of God's Kingdom, is not as important as taking time to simply focus on Jesus. So, there are many things that can draw us away from His presence –

---

[161] Luke 10:40
[162] Luke 10:42

whether pleasure, work, or duty. Only by removing all our distractions for a while can we really be free to focus on God.

At one point early in my current wilderness journey, I told God I felt I had nothing left beyond just the desire for Him. It was not as serenely perfect and holy as that sounds – I was feeling raw and vulnerable, stripped of everything I used to think I knew, and like I had failed. He answered with the following (if you identify with this season, it is for you too):

'Beloved, you are not failing. It is not failure to keep looking to Me while everything around you crumbles. Your fight to hold onto faith and hope in the midst of enemy assault is beautiful. This is not the end, My child. This is just the narrow way – the pinch point that strips you of what is not necessary, and through which you access the wide-open spaces I have prepared for you. Do not be dismayed or discouraged – I have not forgotten you. I did not bring you this far to abandon you now.[163] *You will not fail.'*

(There are several 'do not be dismayed/discouraged' scriptures. I encourage you to look them up: they are very uplifting! Here are a few: Isaiah 41:10; Joshua 1:9; Deuteronomy 31:8; Josh 10:25.)

As God mentioned the pinch point, I could see a picture of a narrow doorway in a wall – like the mythical 'Eye of the Needle' doorway some people used to think Jesus was referring to in Matthew 19:24, where a camel had to be stripped of all it was carrying, then kneel down and crawl through the doorway into the holy city of Jerusalem.

A narrow doorway like this may not seem to have many similarities to a wide-open wilderness, but we need to navigate many narrow valleys and ravines there at times. It is not all wide and exposed: some of our journey may take us to narrow pinch points like these. And this is where we learn to shed all excess baggage that would slow down our progress, just as it would stop a beast of burden squeezing through a tight place. It can be relatively easy to ditch the distractions and stuff we weren't that attached to, but sometimes we also have to lay down many things that were good at one time, or really dear to us and even

---

[163] Philippians 1:6

necessary for our wellbeing, leaving us entirely focused and dependent on God for what is to come.

As Jesus said in Matthew 7:13-14, "Enter through the narrow gate. For wide is the gate and broad is the road that leads to destruction, and many enter through it. But small is the gate and narrow the road that leads to life, and only a few find it."

Like that 'narrow gate', this pinch point is not easy. By necessity we must slow down and come to a complete stop, and then be stripped of everything we've been carrying and relying upon, including all the strengths we thought we had learned as Christians in our lives up to now.

I feel I have been at this pinch point more than once. So, I can only assume there is more stripping required. Every time I feel like I should be doing more, or am failing, that is another layer of self-effort being stripped away; another layer of distraction being removed so I can better focus on Jesus. It is messing with my head because my head does not get it yet. But my heart is increasingly learning to simply and fully look to Jesus. He is, and has finished, everything I will ever need.[164] Anything else is excess baggage.

If you are in a pinch point too, I want to encourage you today: this is not the end. If your eyes are still on Jesus, you have not failed. You *are* overcoming, regardless of how it feels, so keep focusing on Him. Yes, we are weak – we have NOTHING of value to offer. But the more we embrace that, the better positioned we truly are to see His power displayed.

---

[164] 2 Peter 1:3

Chapter 37 – Place of BARRENNESS

"Where is the L<small>ORD</small>, who brought us up out of Egypt
and led us through the barren wilderness,
through a land of deserts and ravines, a land of drought
and utter darkness…"
Jeremiah 2:6

O<small>UT OF ALL</small> the associated characteristics of a wilderness, one of the main distinguishing features mentioned in the Bible is that of barrenness. Typically, these are uncultivated, inhospitable environments that bear little to no fruit. In contrast, gardens (like the Garden of Gethsemane, known for producing olives) are well looked after – tended carefully to keep them free from rocks and weeds, and watered frequently so they can bear fruit. But the wilderness environment is too hostile, rocky, and dry for anything to grow and flourish except for the most scrubby and thorny bushes. Barrenness – or fruitlessness – is a result of the Fall,[165] which resulted in humankind being cursed to struggle to produce food from a barren land.

Of course, barrenness does not only apply to the land around us. There is at least one other kind of fruitlessness. As I shared in *Friend of God,* I have personal experience of being barren. After trying to conceive for a couple of years, my husband and I were told by reproductive specialists that we had next to no chance of doing so

---

[165] Genesis 3:17-18

naturally, and even with IVF the chances were slim. Thankfully, God intervened and helped us to conceive supernaturally, but that was only after almost seven years of barrenness. I am well acquainted with the pain, frustration, deep disappointment, and aching emptiness associated with this condition.

And, just as barrenness manifests physically in desert lands or childless wombs, so it also presents in our spiritual lives. When we go through wilderness seasons, one of the painfully frustrating symptoms we experience is a lack of fruit in our spiritual life. Once we might have read our Bible and found it living and active, bringing fresh revelation and application to our walk with God. But in harder seasons it can feel dry and dusty – far removed from our daily life. Maybe when we used to pray, we experienced the joyful communion of relationship with God, sensing His loving presence and receiving guidance from Him. But in the wilderness, we lose that consciousness of His presence, and our prayers feel feeble, ineffective, and pointless. In better times we dream and take steps of faith, reaching out to those around us, ministering love, grace, and hope. But when the free flow of the Holy Spirit seems to dry up, it all feels worthless, and we cannot see any fruit. 'What's the point?' we ask ourselves, feeling useless for having achieved nothing of value that we can see. Human beings were created in the image of the Creator: made to create and reproduce; made to make a difference. Barrenness stops us doing what we were made for. It is immensely discouraging and depressing.

But we know Jesus promised that in this life we would have trouble.[166] Nobody has a problem-free life. And just like every other difficulty in life, especially the wilderness, God provides the solution. He allows the dryness and barrenness so that we will recognise Him when – not if – He breaks through. Because He is the God who makes the barren woman to be a joyful mother of children;[167] He is the God who makes rivers run on barren heights and produces pools of water in the desert;[168] He is the God who allows weeping to remain for a

---

[166] John 16:33
[167] Psalm 113:9 NKJV
[168] Isaiah 41:18

night but always brings joy in the morning.[169] He is the faithful gardener of our lives, who does not leave us to become a permanent wilderness forever but causes blooms to grow: His Holy Spirit is a wellspring of life that waters us continually. Like we saw in Chapter 35, the dry conditions around us are temporary, allowed only to cause us to put down deeper roots.

Once, I was feeling discouraged about a perceived lack of fruit in my life. I felt my attempts to follow the Holy Spirit's guidance were not achieving anything, and I wondered aloud to God if I had heard His leading right, or if I was bearing no fruit – in a barren wilderness – because I had gone wrong somewhere. His answer was a correction, but utterly encouraging. He said, *'You are looking for the wrong fruit.'* And immediately I saw a picture of two plants side by side – an apple tree and a grapevine. I did a little research, and it confirmed what I felt God was saying. Grapevines take up to about three years to grow from seed to fruit-bearing plant, while apple trees take about seven to ten. God was showing me He had planted a metaphorical apple tree in me that He was nurturing, and that ultimately it would bear much fruit that would last for generations. But it was like I had got to the three-year mark and was comparing it with the vine, seeing abundant fruit on that but none on myself, causing me to feel frustrated and inadequate. God said, *'Three-year-old apple trees are not ready to bear fruit – it isn't time. But the fruit will come if you don't give up.'*[170]

So, I want to encourage you today. You may be in a season of barrenness where you have been faithfully doing everything you know to do, and it still does not seem to be bearing fruit. But God will not leave you in that place. Jesus came that you might have life in abundance.[171] His Spirit is a wellspring of life within you,[172] and as you continue to yield to Him, you won't be able to help bearing fruit.[173] It just might be that God is growing apples in you, not grapes. So do not

---

[169] Psalm 30:5
[170] Galatians 6:9
[171] John 10:10
[172] John 4:13-14
[173] Galatians 5:22-25

be discouraged if you cannot see fruit right now – it will come, and God will be glorified even more because this wilderness season will have taught you that it was not of your doing, only His.

Chapter 38 – Place of
TRANSFORMATION

*"(When) the Spirit from heaven is poured out on us… the
desert will become an orchard, and the orchard will seem
like a forest."*
Isaiah 32:15 (HCSB)

FOLLOWING ON FROM yesterday's chapter about fruitfulness coming to barren lands, let's take some more time to reflect on how God transforms the wilderness. So many scriptures describe this I found it hard to pick just one.

For example, Isaiah 43:19 – "See, I am doing a new thing! Now it springs up; do you not perceive it? I am making a way in the wilderness and streams in the wasteland."

Or Isaiah 51:3 – "The LORD will surely comfort Zion and will look with compassion on all her ruins; he will make her deserts like Eden, her wastelands like the garden of the LORD. Joy and gladness will be found in her, thanksgiving and the sound of singing."

And Psalm 107:35 – "He turned the desert into pools of water and the parched ground into flowing springs."

There are many more. But the one I chose to open this chapter is perhaps my favourite, because it speaks of more than water: it speaks of the fruitfulness that follows it. And the picture of fruitfulness in this translation is a huge, fruitful orchard. As we saw, apple trees do not spring up overnight: from being planted as a seed to being a tree mature enough to bear fruit, it takes about seven to ten years. And this verse is not just about a single fruitful tree, but rather so many fruitful trees that the orchard is like a great forest! Forests of mature, fruit-bearing trees are about as far-removed from a dry and barren wilderness as I can imagine.

It can be almost impossible to consider ever getting to this state of fruit-bearing life when we are in a desert. But nothing is impossible with God.[174] And our opening verse is clear about the reason for the transformation: it's new life from Heaven, or in other translations, specifically the Holy Spirit. Because only God can work this kind of radical, 180° change from desert to rivers, barrenness to fruitfulness, mourning to joy,[175] ashes to beauty, and despair to praise.[176]

And we can rest assured that He is not just going to leave us in the wilderness: He is committed to working that kind of transformation within each of us.[177] But just as a desert does not turn into a forest of fruit trees overnight, sometimes we must surrender to the process of change. It reminds me of a picture God clearly showed me back in the first 2020 lockdown, of a butterfly cocoon: the place where a caterpillar is enclosed in a safe but isolated place so it can undergo the process of metamorphosis, transformed from one state of being into an entirely different one.

A caterpillar is basically a walking stomach: its entire purpose and physiology is designed to access and eat as much food as possible, to grow big and strong before the cocooning process. However, once it becomes a butterfly its purpose is now reproduction: its stomach is much smaller, but it now has reproductive organs and beautiful wings for flying.

And what I felt God say to me was this: *Make the most of this season to come away with Me – it is a season of uncomfortable process. You have been like a caterpillar that has been eating and eating – consuming until fit to burst – and have now entered a hidden cocoon of isolation where no*

---

[174] Luke 1:37 NKJV
[175] Psalm 30:11-12
[176] Isaiah 61:3
[177] Philippians 1:6

one but I can see the secret process that transforms My people from greedy little earthbound caterpillars into glorious butterflies, designed to reflect My beauty, to reproduce, and to fly!

'Trust Me in this season, beloved. As the caterpillar inside a chrysalis turns to mush and the old skin is removed, only its DNA is left intact as it is re-formed. It is not a comfortable process and will leave you feeling as if you do not know which way is up. But it is My designed process, and I will bring you to greater joy and freedom. The time is almost here for you to spread your wings and fly!'

Sometimes it is clearly God who leads us into wilderness seasons (like the Holy Spirit leading Jesus there in Matthew 4). But some of the things that lead us here are not of God. If we are here through bereavement, sickness, or persecution, for example – those are not from Him. It is the enemy who comes to steal, kill, and destroy, not God, whose plans for us are always good. But still, He can and will use anything we go through to strengthen us if we will turn to Him. When we remember He is with us and trust Him to transform us even when we feel like mush, we can be sure He is working all things together for our good.[178] And I firmly believe He is working something good right now, even if we might sometimes feel like we do not know which way is up.

When transformation comes, we always have a choice over how we respond: we can fight it – complaining, seeking the comfort we used to know, and trying to get ourselves out as quickly as possible (which could leave us vulnerable and exposed); we can descend into self-pity, feeling like a victim (which could leave us with no strength to emerge from our chrysalis when the time is over); or we can turn to God in honesty – bringing even the complaints and self-pity that may arise – and seek His path through. It may take us to surprising places. His path may not be the most direct route (remember the Israelites?) but when we trust Him, we can be sure He *will* use the time to transform us in such a way that we bear maximum fruit. That is when we become beautiful butterflies. That is when our dry and difficult times end up

---

[178] Romans 8:28

becoming whole forests of fruit-bearing trees. It sounds like a good deal to me!

Chapter 39 – Place of BURNOUT

"(Elijah) went a day's journey into the wilderness. He came to a broom bush, sat down under it and prayed that he might die. 'I have had enough, LORD,' he said. 'Take my life; I am no better than my ancestors.'"

1 Kings 19:4

IN THIS CHAPTER's opening verse, Elijah had just experienced the great showdown on Mount Carmel when he proved to all Israel that God was greater than Baal and then had the idol-worshipping prophets executed. Following that, he prayed intensely for rain seven times until it arrived, ending a lengthy national drought, and *then* he outran King Ahab's horse-drawn chariot for fifteen miles. What a day! What victory! We might think he would have been on a real high after experiencing God's power so mightily. But it was not so. Many ministers will be familiar with the exhaustion that follows times of ministry (that caused even Jesus to need to retreat to the wilderness for prayer). And on top of this, Elijah had Ahab's wife, Queen Jezebel, vowing to kill him in revenge for his actions against her 'prophets'. So Elijah, no doubt wearied by the intensity of his ministry, became afraid and immensely discouraged, praying to die.

In wilderness seasons, the dry and lonely environment around us can make feelings of exhaustion, fear, and isolation seem even worse. I have experienced this kind of lonely hopelessness, and I know how hard it is to overcome. We know we need to pray, declare God's Word, or sing songs of praise to push back the darkness. But when we are burnt out, sometimes we do not even have the strength for those things – we can't do anything but rest.

And that is why I love this part of Elijah's story so much. He was not just a mighty man of God, or a powerful prophet – though he was clearly both of those – he was also a human, just like us,[179] with very human needs and responses. And when he was at his most needy, God did not tell him to pull himself together, man up, push through, or anything that we might consider. No, He sent an angel to give him some food and tell him to sleep. And once Elijah had slept, the angel returned with more food, knowing that his physical needs were just as important as his spiritual ministry. The angel said, "The journey is too much for you."[180]

It can be an easy mistake to make, especially for those not in a wilderness season right now, to over-spiritualise these seasons and try to make all our pain, suffering, and loneliness feel like distant, irrelevant inconveniencies. But God knows. As we have read in other chapters, He sees and understands – Jesus even experienced it Himself. He knows our pain and struggles; He knows the exhausting loneliness that can come when we are doing our best to serve Him but still suffer. He KNOWS. And sometimes His solution is beautifully, humanly practical: take a nap; have a snack; rest and regain strength.

For Elijah was at the end of himself. He had absolutely no strength left and felt like it was all over: he was done. But God was not finished with him. In that wilderness place where there were no people around either to help or distract, God tended to Elijah's practical needs and restored him, ready to send him on the next mission. He had more work for Elijah to do (including the anointing of his successor), and He knew Elijah *would* be up for it again – he just needed to catch his breath and get his strength back.

When we find ourselves in that place – exhausted, having lost sight of hope, and utterly discouraged, let's be sure to be as kind to ourselves

---

[179] James 5:17
[180] 1 Kings 19:7

as God is. It is not self-indulgent to recognise when we are burnt out; it is vital. So, we must allow ourselves to rest and feed our bodies with plenty of sleep and nourishing food. And then rest some more – for as long as it takes. If we try to rush the process it will not work. And as we do not all have angels manifesting before us to care for our needs, it is also a good idea to check in with a trusted friend or mentor so they can help us assess how we're doing, until such time as we feel ready to run with Jesus again.

I have heard sermons preached on how Elijah was depressed at this point, and suicidal. Certainly, he does seem depressed in the kind of way brought on by circumstances like intense exhaustion and prolonged opposition. And his prayer to God to take his life could be seen as suicidal. But he did not act on it – he did not attempt to take his own life. So personally, I am not sure how helpful it is to use his example as a comparison for those suffering from clinical depression and/or suicidal ideation, as the implication could be that if someone does not feel better after a snack and a nap, they're out of options. And that is just not true.

There are many precious people on the planet struggling with these and other related mental health issues, and if you are one of them, I want to reach out a hand and say you are not alone. You have not failed as a Christian, and you are not letting God or anyone else down. God passionately loves you. He sees your pain, and His compassion is for you. He wants to help you – yes, through prayer and relationship with Him, but also through those He has placed around you who are able to help. Fighting mental health issues is as much a battle as fighting physical illness – it is usually less visible, but every bit as important to be supported through it. So, talking to friends or family is important, where possible. Do not let fear of burdening them put you off – those who love you will want to offer support. And do use the professional services around you too: talk to your doctor and take medication if prescribed; phone helplines such as the Samaritans[181] however often you need to; seek counselling by a qualified practitioner for help in

---

[181] Samaritans phone no: 116 123

addressing any root causes. And meanwhile have friends or prayer teams praying for the effectiveness of all the above. You are not meant to fight this alone.

Chapter 40 – Place of TURNAROUND

*"Then the Lord said to Joshua, 'Today I have rolled away from
you the shame of Egypt.' So the name of that place is called
Gilgal to this day. The people of Israel stayed at Gilgal. They
kept the Passover on the evening of the fourteenth day of the
month on the desert plains of Jericho."*
Joshua 5:9-10 (NLV)

T HE NATION OF Israel had lived as vagabonds in the wilderness
for forty years. They had been there so long that all but two of
the generation who escaped Egypt eventually died in the
desert. We know that the reason for Israel living in the wilderness for
so long was that ten out of twelve spies in the early days reacted in fear
when they went to check out the land promised to them by God, and
that fear quickly infected the whole nation. Even though Israel were
now physically and geographically freed from Egypt, the associated
stink of weakness, hopelessness, and fear clung to them still. The weeks
of miraculous plagues and signs had been exciting and impressive, but
they had generations of experience as slaves, so lived according to what
they knew rather than God's promise. And so, they lived forty years in
the wilderness until the generation of fear-filled, hope-less Israelites
died off and were replaced by a new people who had never known
slavery, only desert living. It took a relatively short time for God to get
Israel out of Egypt, but it then took forty years in the wilderness to get
Egypt out of Israel's collective mindset. It makes me wonder if God

brings us all to the wilderness to deliver us from old enslaving mindsets too… it seems very likely.

Eventually there were no individuals left in Israel who identified as refugees from slavery. All that was left was a nation of desert nomads with no home of their own, only a promised dream. Now freed from the old, but not yet released into the new. Still wandering in a dry and barren land even after the fear and stain of Egypt was purged from among them. Did their wilderness seem endless? Pointless? Or had they made their peace with it? After all, it was the only life they knew to live.

Then the day came when the season changed. Moses' death must have given some of them a hint that a season of change was upon them, but even though he had told them they would possess the land beyond the Jordan, they cannot have fully known what to expect: wilderness living was all they knew; this dry and weary land had become their identity. Even miraculous manna can lose its wonder when it is all you have known.

When we have been deprived for any length of time, it can be hard to remember how it once felt to have anything else. Even while longing for the dry and dusty season to come to an end, it can feel impossible to envision anything other than lack and difficulty. But God knows what good things are ahead for us, just as He knew what was ahead for Israel. He had already planned for a whole new generation of Israelites to pass through the Jordan River as He miraculously parted it for them. And with two bookends of miraculous deliverance through water into and out of the wilderness – two generations baptised into new beginnings through either the Red Sea or the Jordan – the Promised Land season was about to begin. But did Israel know that? And if they did know, did they understand? I doubt it.

Lately I have seen a few signs and received a few words that seem to be saying my wilderness season is coming to an end. It's exciting but also terrifying. Do I dare to hope? How will I handle whatever comes next? I have made my peace with this place; I know how to depend on God here – will I lose that when I come into a more fresh and fruitful season? I don't want to go back to how I was before – God has set me free from so much here – but what else could be next? There are so many unknowns that my exhausted soul does not know what to do with it all. I wonder if the Israelites felt like that too: sensing the Promised Land was almost within grasp, although still with no clear way ahead, and unable to identify with anything other than the desert. When even the dry wilderness has become familiar, it takes real faith to step into a new unknown.

So, God led me to read about Israel at Gilgal, and the significance of its name, given in response to God's promise to Israel made there: "Then the Lord said to Joshua, 'Today I have rolled away the reproach of Egypt from you.' So the place has been called Gilgal (which means 'rolling') to this day."[182]

Gilgal was the place they camped immediately after crossing the Jordan. At Gilgal they paused and circumcised the whole generation born in the desert.[183] And it was at that point of renewed covenant when God spoke and told them He was turning it all around: no longer would they identify with the shame of slavery in Egypt, or even their association with the wilderness – they were coming into their own land for the first time in four hundred and forty years! Gilgal – the rolling place – was their place of turnaround.

Whether they realised it right away or not, from this place they were now positioned to enter the Promised Land. One night they were camped by a river – a nation of ex-slaves and wandering vagabonds. The next, God turned it around, rolled away the old association and positioned them for the new. They still had battles to fight and victories to celebrate, but their identity had changed. And Gilgal – still technically the desert that they had lived in for decades – was their place of turning.

One day, what feels like another day in the wilderness will be our last day here. The old will have been purged and we will be positioned for the new. Because the thing about every wilderness experience is that

---

[182] Joshua 5:9
[183] Joshua 5:4-5

they all end. One day we will wake up and it will be time to take the Promised Land, and just like that, we will be released into what's next – no looking back.

So, for those readers who are still in this desert place, feeling the ongoing struggle that although you have come to the end of this book, your own experience continues, I just want to leave you with a couple of thoughts.

After Israel entered the Promised Land and the days of warfare that followed, I do wonder if any of them ever looked back with nostalgia at the simplicity of their desert-dwelling days when all their food and clothing were miraculously provided and God Himself led them with fire and cloud. Did it take hindsight for them to recognise the blessings they had been given?

Today, still (at the point of writing) in a wilderness that has lasted years, I am trying to make the most of the benefits to be found here, in this stripped-down place where I am fully, painfully – but also gratefully – aware of my dependence on God. The next season will arrive in time, bringing new and different challenges, so I am doing my best to submit to this season – and encourage you to do the same. Just please don't expect it to feel glowingly holy – in my experience it does not; it feels brutal. But if we keep our gaze turned to God to transform us here and bring us out, this wilderness will prove to be incredibly good.

It is my sincere hope and prayer – and reason for writing – that this book has helped you to find some pools of blessing in your own wilderness time. If you are still struggling, though, I do encourage you to reach out to trusted and mature Christian friends who will pray for you. And if nobody comes to mind, I will gladly pray for you myself. Just use the contact form on my website, rachelyarworthwriter.uk, and I will be praying for you.

Appendix 1: Hearing God's Voice

Throughout this book I have shared examples of when I believe God spoke to me. If you are following Jesus, God can – indeed He wants to – speak to you too. Jesus said, "My sheep listen to my voice; I know them, and they follow me."[184] And that when the Holy Spirit came, "He will guide you into all the truth. He will not speak on his own; He will speak only what He hears."[185] We know the Holy Spirit descended at Pentecost to fill us, and as He has never left, we know He is still in us today, still speaking truth to all who belong to Him.

It is not always easy to hear Him, though. If you have read Chapter 12, you may remember the 'still small voice' that seems to come from within, that we need to learn to distinguish from all the other 'voices' inside (not literal but metaphorical voices: those of our physical needs, of our own thoughts and opinions, the voice of temptation etc.). Especially when you are learning to hear God's voice it can be confusing figuring out what bits are from God and what is something else. So here are some tips I have learned over time to help you sift and work out the parts that could be from God:

- *Does it line up with Scripture?*
  God's Word is eternally true and does not contradict itself. (Occasionally there are passages that seem to say

---

[184] John 10:27
[185] John 16:13

opposite things, but we usually find on studying them more deeply that there is a deeper truth that covers both.) In terms of testing the words we receive, God's written Word is the best benchmark, and the more you study your Bible to better know and understand it, the better equipped you will be to check what you hear.

- *Does it line up with God's true character?*
  The more we read our Bibles, the more we learn God is a loving Father: faithful, true, unchanging, forgiving, just, patient, and kind. If the words you are hearing make you feel condemned or afraid, that is not God's voice. Even when God does correct us, He does it lovingly to restore us. Thanks to Jesus, we are no longer under condemnation.[186]

- *Does the Holy Spirit within you witness to its truth?*
  All Spirit-filled Christians have God Himself living inside them, and with practice you will get used to His guidance. But don't let that be your only test. Do not accept/reject words based solely on a feeling, however 'spiritual' it seems. None of us are deception-proof – we all have blind spots. So, remember to ask the other questions too.

- *Do other trusted Spirit-filled Christians agree?*
  Especially when you are learning to hear God's voice, it is helpful to seek input from those who have experience in this area, as they will help you to mature in hearing and discerning. But bear in mind that we are all fallible and even Spirit-filled Christians do not always agree, so this is meant to be a support, not a substitute for developing your own ability to discern.

---

[186] Romans 8:1

If you are still not sure, or some of it feels a little confusing, ask God to confirm it to you more clearly (confusion is not from Him, and He is always happy to give wisdom to those who ask for it.)[187] We often have to sift His words from our own emotions and opinions, so do continue to seek clarity over which are the important parts for you. And wherever possible, study the subject in the Bible, asking God to bring clarity through His written word.

---

[187] James 1:5

Appendix 2: On Fasting

THERE ARE MANY ways to fast. Some Christians believe the only 'proper' way to fast is by giving up food entirely for forty days as Jesus did. If God calls you to that, I am sure it will be hard, but also a real blessing: you will learn to lean on Him more than ever. But contrary to what I have heard preached by some, there is not just one 'right' way to fast. This is especially important for those who have good reason not to fast (e.g. pregnant women, diabetics, children, those with eating disorders or other medical issues). In the Bible many forms of fasting are recorded: different lengths, types, and reasons for it – see examples below. And in our modern lives there are even more forms of fasting that can be helpful, even though they would not have existed in Bible times, e.g. fasting things like TV/social media, which can really help in seasons where you want to shut out distractions and listen to God's voice. So, it is vitally important to ask the Holy Spirit to lead you in the fast HE is calling you to. And remember, fasting is not just for Lent: God can – and will – lead you to it at any time.

Personal Examples:

I first attempted a forty-day water-only fast in my twenties, as part of a corporate fast that some people from my church were doing and I wanted to join in. I managed only a few days before becoming very weak and faint. Some might suggest I should have pushed through as I was probably experiencing the detox that naturally happens around that stage of a water-only fast, and that God would have given me the grace to continue. That may be true for some, but God did not tell me to continue, so for me to have done so would not have been faith, but presumption. Instead, when I prayed about it, I felt He led me to do a liquid-only fast for the remainder of the forty days: I lived on just soups and juices. That still required a huge amount of self-denial that led to breakthrough, and it was an important lesson to always ask God first what fast HE is calling me to.

Since then, I have undertaken many fasts at various times, from full (water-only) fasts, to going without things unrelated to food. There was the time I went without food every Tuesday and Friday for an entire year for a specific cause. At other times I have fasted (water only) every other day for several weeks, seeking breakthrough. I have also fasted from sunrise to sundown for a period of weeks by only eating one main meal every evening so I could give the other mealtimes over to prayer instead of eating.

And it is not just about food: I periodically have times of fasting things like social media, just to focus on God's voice. During lockdown I felt led to fast from all Christian books except the Bible. I even fasted from talking at one time because I felt God led me to – it was a great time that really helped me to listen more.

The point is not to get legalistic about it (if the word 'should' appears in your thought process, that could well be a sign of legalism). If you feel drawn to fasting, simply seek the guidance of the Holy Spirit – what is He asking you to go without, how often and for how long, and for what reason? (Sometimes He may not give you an obvious reason, but it can help if you do have a specific focus.) Then obey Him IN FAITH, trusting that He has a good plan and purpose for what He is leading you to undertake.

Biblical Examples:

Lengths of fast

1 day (sunrise to sunset) – Judges 20:26
(Modern Jews still observe some fasts that abstain from food between sunrise and sundown only, while other fasts are for twenty-four hours from sundown to sundown the next day.)
3 days – Esther 4:16; Acts 9:9
7 days – 1 Samuel 31:13
10 days – Daniel 1:12
14 days – Acts 27:33-34
21 days – Daniel 10:3
40 days – Exodus 34:28; 1 Kings 19:8; Matthew 4:2-4

Types of fast

No food or water* – Deuteronomy 9:9; Esther 4:16
No food – Matthew 4:2
Restricted food – Daniel 1:12
Other restricted activities – 1 Corinthians 7:5
Please don't try to restrict water without medical advice – it can damage your body.

Reasons for fasting

Seeking God – Deuteronomy 9:9
Mourning – Joel 2:12
Seeking help – 2 Chronicles 20:3-4
Seeking wisdom/guidance, and dedication – Acts 14:23
Seeking protection – Ezra 8:21
Seeking breakthrough and favour – Esther 4:16
Spiritual growth – Mark 9:29 NKJV

PS One of the things I appreciate about fasting is how grateful it makes us for food, treats and so on afterwards. God has often used the end of a fast to invite me into a season of feasting in faith, to bring balance and a healthy sense of celebration, gratitude, and rejoicing. Pride in any achievement of self-denial is an easy trap to fall into after completing a fast – it can quickly become self-righteousness, which is no better than idol-worship. So, I fully endorse seasons of feasting too, if it is God who leads us to them. Let us make the most of the fasts we are called to, but also enjoy the 'fatness' and seasons of rejoicing that He sends, in faith that it is GOD alone who makes us holy and gives us breakthrough, never our own efforts.

Appendix 3: Who I am in Christ

This is not an exhaustive list but will get you started. I encourage you to use a good Bible search app (e.g. BibleHub.com) to search for more scriptures on this theme.

I am...

Accepted

The glory of His grace, by which He made us accepted in the Beloved. (Ephesians 1:6 NKJV)

Being transformed into the image of Christ

The Lord – who is the Spirit – makes us more and more like him as we are changed into his glorious image. (2 Corinthians 3:18 NLT)

A Child of God

In Christ Jesus you are all children of God through faith. (Galatians 3:26)

Forgiven

If we confess our sins, he is faithful and just and will forgive us our sins and purify us from all unrighteousness. (1 John 1:9)

Free

It is for freedom that Christ has set us free. (Galatians 5:1)

Fully loved

I am convinced that nothing can ever separate us from God's love. Neither death nor life, neither angels nor demons, neither our fears for today nor our worries about tomorrow—not even the powers of hell can separate us from God's love. No power in the sky above or in the earth below—indeed, nothing in all creation will ever be able to separate us from the love of God that is revealed in Christ Jesus our Lord. (Romans 8:38-39 NLT)

A New Creation

This means that anyone who belongs to Christ has become a new person. The old life is gone; a new life has begun! (2 Corinthians 5:17 NLT)

Made Righteous

This righteousness is given through faith in Jesus Christ to all who believe. (Romans 3:22)

Acknowledgements

THE MORE BOOKS I write, the more I appreciate the writing community that I am blessed to be part of and the family and friends God has placed around me. It is no exaggeration to say I could not have done this without you all.

So, my very sincere thanks go to Liz Carter of Capstone Publishing Services – for her gorgeous cover design and excellent proof-reading, line-editing, and formatting skills. Yet again you have turned my efforts into something beautiful, and I am hugely grateful. Also, my deep thanks go to my brilliant beta-readers: Joy Margetts, Jenny Sanders, Alex Banwell, Joy Vee, Natasha Woodcraft and Cath Hensby. I am not sure how I ever managed to gain the friendship and willing help of such experienced writers, but I thank God for each one of you who generously gave your time to make my book better than I could. And similarly, I want to thank Chris Horton for giving his time to keep an expert eye on my theology and make sure I don't say anything heretical or misleading that could cause people to stumble. Thanks, Chris – I really appreciate your friendship and wisdom!

Thank you also to the writing communities who continue to give encouragement, support, and technical advice – particularly the Kingdom Story Writers and the Association of Christian Writers: you all rock!

And to my family and friends who unfailingly believe in me, cheer me on, forgive me when I get distracted by writing, and who pray for me when I get stuck: Mike, Josh, Ben, and Daniel – you make everything worthwhile. And Mum, Aimee, Thelma and Norman, Ro, and Anne – your words of encouragement continue to be a strength and a joy. Thank you all for being the blessings you are.

Finally, to all those who have ever read any of my books, left reviews on Amazon, subscribed to my writer's website or my *In The Secret Place* blog, followed me on Facebook, Instagram or Goodreads, and/or liked or replied to anything I have written… thank you for your support. It may seem small to you, but it means a lot to me, and there were times when I think I would have quit if it were not for you.

Thank You, God, for all these beautiful people You have surrounded me with. Bless them richly as they have blessed me, I pray.